THE HIGHER CRITICISM OF
THE PENTATEUCH

THE HIGHER CRITICISM OF
THE PENTATEUCH

WILLIAM HENRY GREEN, D.D., LL.D.

PROFESSOR OF ORIENTAL AND OLD TESTAMENT LITERATURE IN PRINCETON
THEOLOGICAL SEMINARY

Introduction by
RONALD YOUNGBLOOD

BAKER BOOK HOUSE
Grand Rapids, Michigan

Reprinted from the 1895 edition
published by Charles Scribner's Sons.
Paperback edition issued 1978
by Baker Book House
ISBN: 0-8010-3723-9

Introduction by Ronald Youngblood
copyrighted 1978 by
Baker Book House Company

PHOTOLITHOPRINTED BY CUSHING - MALLOY, INC.
ANN ARBOR, MICHIGAN, UNITED STATES OF AMERICA
1978

INTRODUCTION

WITH the publication of Julius Wellhausen's *Die Composition des Hexateuchs* (1876) and *Prolegomena zur Geschichte Israels* (1878), the liberal higher criticism of the Pentateuch reached its structural and philosophical zenith. Improvements (so called) and modifications would be made in future years, of course. But the documentary hypothesis with respect to Pentateuchal origins would be forever linked with the name of its most brilliant exponent, so much so that the theory itself would become popularly known as the "Wellhausen hypothesis."

It is to the credit of Baker Book House, then, that they have chosen the centenary year of the first edition of Wellhausen's *Geschichte* to reissue one of its most incisive rebuttals, *The Higher Criticism of the Pentateuch* by William Henry Green. A widely accepted conservative response to Wellhausen from the outset, Green's *Criticism* is a closely reasoned critique that still awaits a decisive rejoinder. The book is spare in argument as well as length, but its genius lies precisely in its conciseness. Green has met Wellhausen on his own ground and has answered him, point by point, with devastating effectiveness.

Like Wellhausen, William Henry Green (1825–1896) was a scholar of formidable talent and prodigious industry. Educated at Lafayette College and Princeton Theological Seminary, Green taught Hebrew at Princeton from 1846 to 1849. He was the pastor of Central Presbyterian Church, Philadelphia, from 1849 to 1851 and then returned to teach Oriental and Old Testament literature at Princeton for the last forty-five years of his life. He chaired the American Old Testament Company of the Anglo-American Bible Revision Committee. Because teaching was his first love, he declined to become president of Princeton College when the position was offered to him in 1868. Among his many writings the best-known volumes are perhaps his commentary on the Song of Solomon in the series edited by J. P. Lange (1870), *The Argument of the Book of Job Unfolded* (1874), *Prophets and Prophecy* (1888), *The Old Testament Canon* (1889), *The Unity of the Book of Genesis* (1895), a two-volume *General Introduction to the Old Testament* (published posthumously, 1898–1899) and, of course, *The Higher Criticism of the Pentateuch* (1895), considered by many to be his magnum opus.

While the final paragraph of his *Criticism* issues a gentle (if pointed) warning to evangelical scholars, Green was not afraid of the term *higher criticism* as such. He defended it as a methodological tool while at the same time deploring its perversion (pp. xx–xxi). Nor did he fear the presence of a limited number of post-Mosaica in the Pentateuch, as long as they were not attributed to those sections that specifically claimed to originate with Moses (pp. 51–52). But he attacked the unwarranted presuppositions and erroneous conclusions of the documentary hypothesis with relentless thoroughness. Perhaps more than any other evangelical of his generation he demonstrated the fact that wholly satisfactory, conservative answers could be given to questions being raised by liberal higher critics with respect to the origin and nature of the Pentateuch.

More than eighty years of discussion and debate have taken place since Green's classic confrontations, and the reader may wish to be brought up to date before perusing the *Criticism* itself. Many surveys are available, some by conservatives and some by liberals.[1] While both conservative and liberal treat-

---

[1] See, for example, the following: R. K. Harrison, *Introduction to the Old Testament* (Grand Rapids: Eerdmans, 1969), pp. 3–82, 495–541; G. J. Wenham, "Trends in Pentateuchal Criticism Since 1950," *TSF Bulletin* 70 (Autumn 1974): 1–6; Gleason L. Archer, Jr., *A Survey of Old Testament Introduction* (Chicago: Moody, 1964), pp. 73–165; E. B. Smick, "Pentateuch," in *The Zondervan Pictorial Encyclopedia of the Bible,* ed. Merrill C. Tenney, 5 vols. (Grand Rapids: Zondervan, 1975), 4:674–92; H. F.

ments exude competence and confidence, "flux" with respect
to the current status of Pentateuchal studies and "caution" concerning formerly "assured results" are characteristic watch-
words on both sides.

And now to our own brief survey. In agreement with Green,
James Orr set forth the dangers inherent in the documentary
hypothesis by pointing out that it is, "neither in its methods
nor in its results, entitled to the unqualified confidence often
claimed for it. . . . it rests on erroneous fundamental principles, is eaten through with subjectivity, and must, if carried
out to its logical issues—to which, happily, very many do not
carry it—prove subversive to our Christian faith."[2] Needless to
say, not all scholars have shared that viewpoint. Many, in
fact, have been eager to add to the JEDP series that Wellhausen canonized a fifth document (at the very least). Otto
Eissfeldt insisted that J contains a "lay" (L) source, reflecting
the nomadic, Rechabite ideal, showing hostility to the Canaanite
way of life, and originating during the time of Elijah (ninth
century B.C.). Robert H. Pfeiffer preferred to see in parts of
Genesis an Edomite source, which he called S (for "south"
or "Seir"). Georg Fohrer took Eissfeldt to task for his "inaccurate" terminology and posited in Genesis, Exodus, and
Numbers an N ("Nomadic") source whose "basic attitude . . .
is determined by the concepts of (semi)nomadic Israelite

Hahn, *Old Testament in Modern Research* (Philadelphia: Muhlenberg,
1954), pp. 1–43, 185–225; John Bright, "Modern Study of Old Testament
Literature," in *The Bible and the Ancient Near East: Essays in Honor of
William Foxwell Albright*, ed. G. Ernest Wright (Garden City, N.Y.:
Doubleday, 1961), pp. 13–31 (esp. 13–25); C. R. North, "Pentateuchal
Criticism," in *The Old Testament and Modern Study: A Generation of
Discovery and Research*, ed. H. H. Rowley (New York: Oxford University,
1951), pp. 48–83; N. E. Wagner, "Pentateuchal Criticism: No Clear Future,"
Canadian Journal of Theology 13 (1967): 225–32; and R. J. Coggins, "A
Century of Pentateuchal Criticism," *Church Quarterly Review* 166 (1965):
149–61, 413–25.

[2] *The Problem of the Old Testament Considered with Reference to Recent Criticism* (New York: Scribner, 1906), p. xv.

groups."[3] But although adherence to the JEDP framework remains widespread among liberal Old Testament scholars, proposed additions to the basic four documents have found only limited acceptance.

In fact, the number "four" itself is no longer sacrosanct among protagonists of the documentary hypothesis. Paul Volz and Wilhelm Rudolph have stated that there is no valid basis for making out a separate E-source, seriously questioned the validity of maintaining the existence of E and P as storytellers, made them at best an editor (E) and a legislator (P), and affirmed only J as an author.[4] Distinguishing the joins and seams between the "documents" has also become increasingly difficult since the pioneering work of Hermann Gunkel, who in his form-critical *(formgeschichtlich)* approach to the Old Testament stressed the life situation *(Sitz im Leben)* and literary type *(Gattung)* of each pericope in Genesis (with obvious implications for the rest of the Pentateuch as well).[5] Along with Gunkel, members of the so-called "Uppsala school" have emphasized the role of oral tradition in the transmission of biblical literature. This too tends to obscure the neat distinctions between J, E, D, and P (although the oral-tradition approach is not without problems of its own, as its critics are quick to demonstrate). One of Uppsala's foremost representatives, Ivan Engnell, has asserted that the "P work" (Gen.–Num.) and the "D work" or "Deuteronomic history" (Deut.–II Kings) were written down in postexilic times but based on oral traditions. Repetitions, duplications, and the like are to be explained not by different "documents" but by the "epic law of iteration" in oral transmission.[6]

3 Eissfeldt, *Hexateuch-Synopse* (Leipzig: Hinrichs, 1922); Pfeiffer, *Introduction to the Old Testament* (New York: Harper, 1941); Fohrer, *Introduction to the Old Testament*, trans. David E. Green (Nashville: Abingdon, 1968), p. 160.

4 *Der Elohist als Erzähler ein Irrweg der Pentateuchkritik: An der Genesis Erläutert* (Giessen: Töpelmann, 1933).

5 *Die Sagen der Genesis* (Göttingen: Vandenhoeck and Ruprecht, 1901).

6 *A Rigid Scrutiny: Critical Essays on the Old Testament*, ed. and trans.

While we may applaud Engnell's conservative attitude toward
the Masoretic text and his refusal to impose our modern West-
ern ideas of composition and compilation on ancient Near
Eastern literature, the oral-transmission theory with respect to
the Old Testament is unproven and, in the very nature of the
case, unprovable. As K. A. Kitchen has pointed out, oral *dis-
semination* of written information to *contemporaries* was common enough in ancient times, but for *transmission* "of anything important to *posterity,* the Ancient Orient insistently resorted to written rather than oral transmission."[7]

Another highly questionable aspect of Engnell's approach
is his redivision of the traditional Pentateuch-plus-Former-
Prophets into a Tetrateuch-plus-Deuteronomic-History, a schema
often associated also with Martin Noth.[8] Detaching Deuteronomy from what precedes it and adding it to what follows
it flies in the face of II Kings 14:6, which quotes Deuteronomy 24:16 as a divine command "written in the book of
the law of Moses." In so doing, II Kings 14:6 witnesses to
the traditional placement of Deuteronomy as the concluding
book of a five-volume Pentateuch and denies its inclusion in
a "Deuteronomic history," of which II Kings itself is reputed
to be a part. Nor, incidentally, does the "Hexateuch" of Wellhausen, Eissfeldt, and others fare any better; such a reconstruction flatly contradicts the evidence of Joshua 8:31, which
quotes from Exodus 20:25 and Deuteronomy 27:5–6 as a
divine command "written in the book of the law of Moses"
and which, in so doing, excludes Joshua from the books that
precede it. A four-volume "Tetrateuch" or six-volume "Hexateuch" also fails to do justice to Talmudic tradition, which
refers to Genesis through Deuteronomy as "the five fifths
of the Law"; to Samaritan tradition, which held that the Penta-

---

John T. Willis (Nashville: Vanderbilt University, 1969), pp. 50–67.

[7] *Ancient Orient and Old Testament* (Chicago: Inter-Varsity, 1966),
p. 136. Italics mine.

[8] See Noth's *Überlieferungsgeschichtliche Studien,* vol. 1 (Halle: Nie-
meyer, 1943).

teuch alone constituted Scripture (despite the fact that the writings of Joshua, himself a northerner with close associations to Samaritan sanctuaries, might be expected to have been a welcome addition to the Samaritan canon); and to the Hebrew Psalter, whose division into five books is, says Green, "probably patterned after the Pentateuch, and is most likely as old as the constitution of the canon" itself (p. 18).

Although Engnell erroneously claimed that the books of the Pentateuch were not given written form until postexilic times, he has performed a salutary service by reminding us that the books themselves contain materials that are older, and often *much* older, than the time of their reduction to writing. Research in various disciplines since Wellhausen's time has tended more and more to confirm the traditional view that Moses and his contemporaries (or immediate successors) are responsible for virtually the entire Pentateuch as we have it today. William Foxwell Albright, ever the champion of empirical fact as opposed to unfounded hypothesis, asserted that our understanding of ancient Canaanite poetic style as reflected in Ugaritic epic literature makes it necessary for us to date the Song of Miriam (Exod. 15:1–18) to about 1300–1275 B.C., the Oracles of Balaam (Num. 23:7–10, 18–24; 24:3–9, 15–24) to about 1200, the Blessing of Moses (Deut. 33) to about 1050, the Song of Moses (Deut. 32:1–43) to about 1025, and the Blessing of Jacob (Gen. 49:2–27) to slightly later than 1025.[9] It should be noted that these are the *latest* possible dates, based on a particular set of criteria; other considerations may be used to raise at least some of the dates.

In addition to the Ugaritic materials, other epigraphic finds uncovered by archaeologists during the twentieth century also tend to push the dates of specific sections of the Pentateuch further and further back. Legal tablets excavated at Nuzi demonstrate the antiquity of numerous customs and practices cur-

[9] *Yahweh and the Gods of Canaan: A Historical Analysis of Two Contrasting Faiths* (Garden City, N.Y.: Doubleday, 1968), pp. 12, 15, 17, 19.

rent during the patriarchal period (Gen. 12–50). The Hittite laws make it unlikely that Genesis 23 is later than about 1200 B.C.[10] Albrecht Alt observed that the laws of the Pentateuch find their most appropriate context in similar materials uncovered in a wide area of the ancient Near East and dating from the second millennium.[11] Shalom M. Paul has noted that the literary structure of Exodus 19–24 (historical prologue, laws, epilogue containing blessings and curses) is very similar to that of the codes of Lipit-Ishtar (about 1900 B.C.) and Hammurapi (about 1750); it is not unreasonable therefore to date Exodus 19–24 during the time of Moses.[12] George E. Mendenhall has argued that the literary structure of Exodus 20: 1–17 rests on traditions that go back to the international suzerainty covenants of the Hittite Empire (about 1450–1200 B.C.), and Meredith G. Kline has extended Hittite treaty literary influence to the entire book of Deuteronomy, claiming it to be a covenant-renewal document that brings the original stipulations of the Decalogue up to date—but all within the time of Moses.[13] According to M. J. Selman, "all the available parallels to the firstborn's share in Dt. 21:17 come from the third quarter of the second millennium."[14]

Of potentially far greater importance for the age of the Pentateuch in general and of Genesis in particular are the Ebla tablets discovered from 1974 to 1977 at Tell Mardikh in northern Syria. Dating from the late third millennium B.C.— perhaps even as early as 2500—they contain the earliest known references to such Pentateuchal personal names as Abram, Esau, Ishmael, Israel, Michael, and S(h)aul. The king of Ebla was Ebrium, the semantic and linguistic equivalent of Eber

10 See Kitchen, *Ancient Orient and Old Testament*, p. 25.

11 *Die Ursprünge des Israelitischen Rechts* (Leipzig: Hirzel, 1934).

12 *Studies in the Book of the Covenant in the Light of Cuneiform and Biblical Law* (Leiden: Brill, 1970).

13 Mendenhall, *Law and Covenant in Israel and the Ancient Near East* (Pittsburgh: Biblical Colloquium, 1955); Kline, *Treaty of the Great King* (Grand Rapids: Eerdmans, 1963), pp. 20, 28.

14 *Themelios* 3 (1977): 15 (n. 34).

(Gen. 10:26), the ancestor of the Hebrew people. Pentateuchal place-names that appear in the Ebla tablets include
Gaza, Sidon, Jerusalem, and—*mirabile dictu*—Sodom, Gomorrah, Admah, Zeboiim, and Bela, found in exactly the same
order in Genesis 14:2, 8 and on an ordinary Ebla economic
tablet (no. 1860)! On still another Ebla tablet Zoar is said
to belong to the district of Bela, reminding us that Zoar was
Bela's other name (Gen. 14:2, 8). (These parallels to Genesis 14 point to an earlier rather than later date for the
biblical Abraham.) If these preliminary Ebla readings are
confirmed by subsequent research on the tablets, the Tell
Mardikh discoveries·may well revolutionize Pentateuchal scholarship by helping to turn it in a more conservative direction.

Literary studies have tended to modify the late-date propensities of the Wellhausen school. R. K. Harrison has claimed
the Pentateuch to be substantially Mosaic but perhaps revised
and edited during the monarchy, such practices being well
attested elsewhere in the ancient Near East; the Pentateuch
"in virtually its extant form was in existence by the time of
Samuel." In essential agreement with Harrison is G. C. Aalders, who has asserted that Genesis 36:31 could not have been
written before the reign of King Saul. M. H. Segal has said
that the basis of the Pentateuch is Mosaic, although later
amplifications were possible.[15]

With respect to the individual books of the Pentateuch,
Umberto Cassuto has said that Genesis was written late in
the reign of David, but by one author who based his work
on oral traditions, combining them into a unified and harmonious whole.[16] The 621 B.C. date of Deuteronomy (D),
one of the mainstays of the documentary hypothesis, has
nevertheless come under increasing attack on all sides. Gustav

[15] *Introduction to the Old Testament*, p. 541; see also p. 622. Aalders,
A Short Introduction to the Pentateuch (London: Tyndale, 1949), p. 107;
see also pp. 157÷58. Segal, *The Pentateuch: Its Composition and Its
Authorship* (Jerusalem: Magnes, 1967), p. 47.

[16] *La Questione della Genesi* (Firenze: Le Monnier, 1934).

Hölscher dated it after the exile on the basis that a demand for a single sanctuary would have been impracticably idealistic in preexilic times. Robert Hatch Kennett also proposed a late date for D since the law of sacrifice in H (the "Holiness" code of Leviticus), which is closely related to Ezekiel, is earlier than the law of sacrifice in Deuteronomy 12. On the other hand Adam C. Welch dated many of the laws of Deuteronomy during the Solomonic or immediate post-Solomonic period because of their primitive character. Edward Robertson dated D earlier still, feeling that it was composed under Samuel's supervision to be used as a lawbook when the Israelites were united under a king and that it was prefaced by other materials collected from various shrines. G. T. Manley has reaffirmed the essentially Mosaic origin of Deuteronomy in a closely reasoned presentation, though stating that the writer of the narrative sections of Deuteronomy was not Moses himself but an onlooker, possibly one of the "priests the Levites" of Deuteronomy 31:9. J. A. Thompson has said that the earliest material in Deuteronomy goes back to the time of Moses, that "the hand of Moses should be discerned throughout the book, even if it is not possible to decide the extent of editorial work," that it combines written material with oral tradition, and that "it may have assumed somewhat of its present form in the general period of the United Monarchy." Peter C. Craigie prefers the time of Moses or shortly afterward, observes that the scribe is not known, affirms that the author of the major substance of the book is Moses himself, and declares his belief that "the source of the work is God, though its mediation is human." As for Deuteronomy's reputed emphasis on a single, centralized place of worship (with implications for late dating), Segal and others have interpreted "the place" to mean a *succession* of sanctuaries rather than a single sanctuary. An additional embarrassment to adherents of the centralization theory was provided by

Harold M. Wiener, who observed that Deuteronomy 16:21 recognizes and approves a plurality of altars.[17]

Wellhausen's late dating, needless to say, he attributed to the posited documents themselves—especially P, which he characterized as postexilic. This aspect of his hypothesis has fallen on hard times recently, not only as the result of archaeological research (witness, for example, the technical sacrificial terminology of the Ugaritic epics), but also from a literary standpoint. Among those who date P much earlier than Wellhausen did are Yehezkel Kaufmann, Samuel R. Külling, and Moshe Weinfeld. Oswald T. Allis asked a couple of pertinent questions concerning this issue: If P is late, why are there many Levites and few priests in the Pentateuch, but few (available) Levites and many priests in Ezra-Nehemiah? Why is music in worship, which P had known for centuries, said to originate with David rather than with Moses? Torn by such questions and seeing both early and late elements in *all* the posited documents, Johannes Pedersen stated that JE (which he refused to subdivide further), D, and P should be understood as designations of collections that cannot be chronologically arranged but that are, rather, parallel and indicate the many-sided variety that characterized Israelite culture.

[17] Hölscher, "Komposition und Ursprung des Deuteronomiums," *Zeitschrift für die Alttestamentliche Wissenschaft* 40 (1922): 161–255; Kennett, *Old Testament Essays* (Cambridge: University, 1928), p. 49; Welch, *The Code of Deuteronomy: A New Theory of Its Origin* (London: Clarke, 1924), and *Deuteronomy: The Framework to the Code* (London: Oxford University, 1932); Robertson, "The Old Testament Problem: A Reinvestigation," *Together with Two Other Essays* (Manchester: Manchester University, 1950); Manley, *The Book of the Law: Studies in the Date of Deuteronomy* (Grand Rapids: Eerdmans, 1957), p. 162; Thompson, *Deuteronomy: An Introduction and Commentary* (Downers Grove, Ill.: InterVarsity, 1974), pp. 45, 8, 47, 68, respectively; Craigie, *The Book of Deuteronomy* (Grand Rapids: Eerdmans, 1976), pp. 28–29, 77; Segal, *The Pentateuch*, p. 88; Wiener, *Essays in Pentateuchal Criticism* (London: Stock, 1913), p. 13. On the last point, see also Archer, *Old Testament Introduction*, p. 246; and Harrison, *Introduction to the Old Testament*, p. 643.

From a somewhat different perspective we have the opinion
of Alexa Suelzer: "Critics like Wellhausen failed to realize
that the writing of a tradition marks the end of an era, not
the beginning. Although the dates assigned to a document
may be accurate they give no clue to the age of the traditions
described in the document." It is perhaps not surprising then
that Albin van Hoonacker could affirm *both* the documentary hypothesis *and* Moses as the substantial author of the
Pentateuch![18]

Since 1947, however, it has been increasingly difficult to
maintain anything remotely resembling the classical Well-
hausenian documents. The three main types of text (proto-
Masoretic, proto-Samaritan, and proto-Septuagintal) found
among the Dead Sea scrolls—especially the 4Q fragments—
have seriously undermined detailed literary criticism of the
Pentateuch. Furthermore, as Kitchen has reminded us, no
tangible manuscript evidence of the separate existence of the
posited documents has ever been discovered through archaeological means.[19] The "documents" remain what they have been
from the outset—a theory, a hypothesis.

Nor do differences in divine names, variations in language
and style, alleged contradictions and divergences of viewpoint,
duplications and repetitions, or supposed signs of composite
structure lead inexorably to a patchwork of documents put
together—sometimes brilliantly, sometimes clumsily (so the

[18] Kaufmann, *The Religion of Israel from Its Beginnings to the Baby-
lonian Exile*, ed. and trans. Moshe Greenberg (Chicago: University of Chicago, 1960); Külling, *Zur Datierung der "Genesis-P-Stücke": Namentlich
des Kapitels Genesis XVII* (Kampen: Kok, 1964); Weinfeld, *Deuteronomy
and the Deuteronomic School* (Oxford: Clarendon, 1972); Allis, *God
Spake by Moses* (Philadelphia: Presbyterian and Reformed, 1951), pp. 98,
112; Pedersen, *Israel: Its Life and Culture*, 2 vols. (London: Oxford University, 1940); Suelzer, *The Pentateuch: A Study in Salvation History*
(New York: Herder and Herder, 1964), p. 43; van Hoonacker, *De composi-
tione litteraria et de origine Mosaica Hexateuchi disquisitio historico-critica*
(Brussels: Paleis der Academiën, 1949). Van Hoonacker's work was written
at the turn of the century.

[19] *Ancient Orient and Old Testament*, p. 23.

theory goes)—by one or more redactors. B. D. Eerdmans asserted that differences between Masoretic and Septuagintal readings make it impossible to use divine names as a clue to separating the "documents."[20] Different names are used not because they characterize different sources but because they have different nuances of meaning.[21] W. J. Martin has stressed the subjectivity of the stylistic argument and points out that earlier attempts to deny large portions of the Homeric epics to Homer on the basis of language and style are no longer in vogue.[22] We might observe here that the Egyptian *Story of Si-nuhe* contains rough transitions, stylistic infelicities, and the like; but who on that account would declare it an editorial mélange?

Green, using the principles of the documentary theorists, "proves"—tongue in cheek—that the parables of the Prodigal Son and the Good Samaritan are composite accounts (pp. 119–24)! Other clever examples of the same kind are LeRoy Koopman's "exegetical comments" on Lincoln's Gettysburg Address and the unsigned "higher critical study" of "'63 Thanksgiving," the latter a poem by Walter Hearn. Cyrus H. Gordon states the dictum that "any one author will employ different styles for different types of subject matter," then illustrates it with several examples. Cassuto provides us with his now-famous illustration of "Father" and "the professor" to clarify the same argument.[23]

[20] *Die Komposition der Genesis* (Giessen: Töpelmann, 1908), pp. 34–35.

[21] See Cassuto, *The Documentary Hypothesis and the Composition of the Pentateuch,* trans. Israel Abrahams (Jerusalem: Magnes, 1961), p. 31; Cassuto, *A Commentary on the Book of Genesis,* trans. Israel Abrahams, 2 vols. (Jerusalem: Magnes, 1961–1964), 1:87–88; and Manley, *The Book of the Law,* pp. 40–41.

[22] *Stylistic Criteria and the Analysis of the Pentateuch* (London: Tyndale, 1955).

[23] Koopman, "The Stiff-Collar Commentary," *Christianity Today,* 5 November 1965, p. 25; " '63 Thanksgiving': A Higher Critical Study," *His* 24 (March 1964): 6–9; Gordon, "Higher Critics and Forbidden Fruit," *Christianity Today,* 23 November 1959, p. 4; Cassuto, *The Documentary Hypothesis,* pp. 57–58.

The bankruptcy of the documentary theory is perhaps most glaringly revealed when it is forced to invoke the aid of a redactor to bail it out when its criteria do not fit a passage. Modern commentaries on the Pentateuch are strewn with references to these amiable nobodies who have inserted words, phrases, and even verses at will. Green, in a choice paragraph, observes that "the opposite traits of character impliedly ascribed to the redactor, the utterly capricious and irrational conduct imputed to him, and the wanton and aimless manipulation of his authorities, for which no motive can be imagined, tend to make this most important functionary an impossible conception" (p. 87). Cassuto has expressed much the same sentiment: "This method, which establishes a given principle *a priori*, without taking into consideration what is expressly stated in the text, and then, placing the passage upon the Procrustean bed of that principle, hacks off the textual limbs that do not fit into the bed, can hardly be accepted as valid." Elsewhere he has pointed out that alleged contradictions are not explained by calling on a redactor, a process that merely shifts the blame.[24]

Patient and careful exegesis can solve many of the supposed discrepancies in the Pentateuchal accounts. Cassuto himself has shown us how with his brilliant defense of the unity of the flood narrative. Segal has underscored the unitary character of the Exodus plague narratives. Moshe Greenberg feels that perhaps some of the so-called contradictions within the Pentateuchal laws are only superficial and, on closer examination, would disclose finer legal distinctions. Martin, who believes a false understanding of Exodus 6:3 to be a key argument in defense of the documentary hypothesis, suggests a number of equally possible interpretations that demolish that defense.[25]

The unity so evident throughout the Pentateuch—a unity

[24] *The Book of Genesis*, 1:viii; *The Documentary Hypothesis*, p. 67.
[25] *The Book of Genesis*, 2:30–45; Segal, *The Pentateuch*, p. 36; Greenberg, "Some Postulates of Biblical Criminal Law," in *Yehezkel Kaufmann Jubilee Volume*, ed. Menahem Haran (Jerusalem, 1960), pp. 5–28; Martin,

conceded by implication by protagonists of the documentary hypothesis, though they attribute it to one or more redactors— is clearly the product of an overall plan and a single, superintending intelligence. It is Green's contention that Moses, under the inspiration of the Holy Spirit, was the writer or compiler of virtually the entire Pentateuch. The overwhelming witness of Jewish and Christian tradition, of the Pentateuch itself (e.g., Exod. 17:14; 34:27; Num. 33:1–2; Deut. 31:9), of the apostle Paul (e.g., Rom. 10:5; II Cor. 3:15), and of Jesus Christ (see especially John 5:45–47) is in agreement with Green. It is therefore a pleasure for me to take this opportunity of commending his classic study of Pentateuchal origins to a new generation of readers.

RONALD YOUNGBLOOD

Analysis of the Pentateuch, pp. 16–19. On the last point see also Manley, *The Book of the Law*, p. 47; Cassuto, *A Commentary on the Book of Exodus*, trans. Israel Abrahams (Jerusalem: Magnes, 1967), pp. 77–79; and Allis, *God Spake by Moses*, p. 65.

PREFACE

THE Higher Criticism has been of late so associated with extravagant theorizing, and with insidious attacks upon the genuineness and credibility of the books of the Bible that the very term has become an offence to serious minds. It has come to be considered one of the most dangerous forms of infidelity, and in its very nature hostile to revealed truth. And it must be confessed that in the hands of those who are unfriendly to supernatural religion it has proved a potent weapon in the interest of unbelief. Nor has the use made of it by those who, while claiming to be evangelical critics, accept and defend the revolutionary conclusions of the antisupernaturalists, tended to remove the discredit into which it has fallen.

This is not the fault of the Higher Criticism in its genuine sense, however, but of its perversion. Properly speaking it is an inquiry into the origin and character of the writings to which it is applied. It seeks to ascertain by all available means the authors by whom, the time at which, the circumstances under which, and the design with which they were produced. Such investigations, rightly conducted, must prove a most important aid to the understanding and just appreciation of the writings in question.

The books of the Bible have nothing to fear from such investigations, however searching and thorough, and however fearlessly pursued. They can only result in establishing more firmly the truth of the claims, which the

Bible makes for itself, in every particular. The Bible stands upon a rock from which it can never be dislodged.

The genuineness and historical truth of the Books of Moses have been strenuously impugned in the name of the Higher Criticism. It has been claimed as one of its most certain results, scientifically established, that they have been falsely ascribed to Moses, and were in reality produced at a much later period. It is affirmed that the history is by no means reliable and merely records the uncertain and variant traditions of a post-Mosaic age; and that the laws are not those of Moses, but the growth of centuries after his time. All this is demonstrably based on false and sophistical reasoning, which rests on unfounded assumptions and employs weak and inconclusive arguments.

It is the purpose of this volume to show, as briefly and compactly as possible, that the faith of all past ages in respect to the Pentateuch has not been mistaken. It is what it claims to be, and what it has always been believed to be. In the first chapter it is exhibited in its relation to the Old Testament as a whole, of which it is not only the initial portion, but the basis or foundation upon which the entire superstructure reposes; or rather, it contains the germs from which all that follows was developed. In the second, the plan and contents of the Pentateuch are unfolded. It has one theme, which is consistently adhered to, and which is treated with orderly arrangement and upon a carefully considered plan suggestive of a single author. In the third it is shown by a variety of arguments, both external and internal, that this author was Moses. The various forms of opposition to this conclusion are then outlined and separately considered. First, the weakness of the earlier objections from anachronisms and inconsistencies is shown. In the fourth chapter the divisive hypotheses, which have in succession been maintained in opposition to the unity of the Pentateuch, are reviewed and shown to be baseless, and the arguments urged in their support are refuted. In the fifth chapter the genuineness of the laws is defended against the development hypothesis. And in the sixth and last chapter these hypotheses are shown to be radically unbiblical. They are hostile alike to the truth of the Pentateuch and to the supernatural revelation which it contains.

PRINCETON, N. J., August 1, 1895.

TABLE OF CONTENTS

I

II

III

IV

THE HIGHER CRITICISM OF THE PENTATEUCH

I

THE OLD TESTAMENT AND ITS STRUCTURE

THE Old Testament is the volume of God's written revelation prior to the advent of Christ. Its complement is the New Testament, which is God's written revelation since the advent of Christ. The former being immediately addressed to the people of Israel was written in the language of that people, and hence for the most part in Hebrew, a few chapters in Daniel and Ezra and a verse in Jeremiah being in the Jewish Aramean,[1] when the language was in its transition state. This earlier dispensation, which for a temporary purpose was restricted to a single people and a limited territory, was, however, preparatory to the dispensation of the fulness of times, in which God's word was to be carried everywhere and preached to every creature. Accordingly the New Testament was written in Greek, which was then the language of the civilized world.

The Old Testament was composed by many distinct writers, at many different times and in many separate portions, through a period of more than a thousand years from Moses to Malachi. It is not, however, an aggre-

---

[1] Jer. x. 11; Dan. ii. 4–vii. 28; Ezra iv. 7–vi. 18, vii. 12–26 are in Aramean.

1

gate of detached productions without order or method, as the seemingly casual circumstances connected with the origin of its several parts might tempt some to imagine. Nor, on the other hand, are the additions made from time to time of a uniform pattern, as though the separate value of each new revelation consisted merely in the fact that an increment was thereby made to the body of divine truth previously imparted. Upon the lowest view that can possibly be taken of this volume, if it were simply the record of the successive stages of the development of the Hebrew mind, it might be expected to possess an organic structure and to exhibit a gradually unfolding scheme, as art, philosophy, and literature among every people have each its characteristics and laws, which govern its progress and determine the measure and direction of its growth. But rightly viewed as the word of God, communicated to men for his own wise and holy ends, it may with still greater confidence be assumed that the order and symmetry which characterize all the works of the Most High, will be visible here likewise; that the divine skill and intelligence will be conspicuous in the method as well as in the matter of his disclosures ; and that these will be found to be possessed of a structural arrangement in which all the parts are wisely disposed, and stand in clearly defined mutual relations.

The Old Testament is a product of the Spirit of God, wrought out through the instrumentality of many human agents, who were all inspired by him, directed by him, and adapted by him to the accomplishment of his own fixed end.   Here is that unity in multiplicity, that single-ness of aim with diversity of operations, that binding to-gether of separate activities under one superior and con-trolling influence, which guides all to the accomplishment of a predetermined purpose, and allots to each its par-ticular function in reference to it, which is the very conception of a well-arranged organism. There is a divine reason why every part is what it is and where it is; why God spake unto the fathers at precisely those sundry times and in just those divers portions, in which he actually revealed his will. And though this may not in every instance be ascertainable by us, yet careful and reverent study will disclose it not only in its general outlines, but also in a multitude of its minor details; and will show that the transpositions and alterations, which have been proposed as improvements, are dislocations and disfigurements, which mar and deface the well-proportioned whole.

In looking for the evidences of an organic structure in the Scriptures, according to which all its parts are disposed in harmonious unity, and each part stands in a definite and intelligible relation to every other, as well as to the grand design of the whole, it will be necessary to group and classify the particulars, or the student will lose himself in the multiplicity of details, and never rise to any clear conception of the whole. Every fact, every institution, every person, every doctrine, every utterance of the Bible has its place and its function in the general plan. And the evidence of the correctness of any scheme proposed as the plan of the Scriptures will lie mainly in its harmonizing throughout with all these details, giving a rational and satisfactory account of the purpose and design of each and assigning to all their just place and relations. But if one were to occupy himself with these details in the first instance, he would be distracted and confused by their multitude, without the possibility of arriving thus at any clear or satisfactory result.

The first important aid in the process of grouping or classification is afforded by the separate books of which the Scriptures are composed. These are not arbitrary or fortuitous divisions of the sacred text : but their form, dimensions, and contents have been divinely determined. Each represents the special task allotted to one particular organ of the Holy Spirit, either the entire function assigned to him in the general plan, or, in the case where the same inspired penman wrote more than one book of different characters and belonging to different classes, his function in one given sphere or direction. Thus the books of Isaiah, Ezekiel, and Malachi exhibit to us that part in the plan of divine revelation which each of those distinguished servants of God was commissioned to perform. The book of Psalms represents the task allotted to David and the other inspired writers of song in the instruction and edification of the people of God. The books of Moses may be said to have led the way in every branch of sacred composition, in history (Genesis), in legislation (Leviticus), in oratorical and prophetic discourse (Deuteronomy), in poetry (Ex. xv., Dt. xxxii., xxxiii.), and they severally set forth what he was engaged to accomplish in each of these different directions. The books of Scripture thus having each an individual character and this stamped with divine authority as an element of fitness for their particular place and function, must be regarded as organic parts of the whole.

The next step in our inquiry is to classify and arrange the books themselves. Every distribution is not a true classification, as a mechanical division of an animal body is not a dissection, and every classification will not exhibit the organic structure of which we are in quest. The books of the Bible may be variously divided with respect to matters merely extraneous and contingent, and which stand in no relation to the true principle of its construction.

Thus, for example, the current division of the Hebrew Bible is into three parts, the Law, the Prophets, and the K'thubhim or Hagiographa. This distribution rests upon the official standing of the writers. The writings of Moses, the great lawgiver and mediator of God's covenant with Israel, whose position in the theocracy was altogether unique, stand first. Then follow the writings of the prophets, that is to say, of those invested with the prophetical office. Some of these writings, the so-called former prophets—Joshua, Judges, Samuel, and Kings— are historical; the others are prophetical, viz., those denominated the latter prophets—Isaiah, Jeremiah, Ezekiel, and the twelve minor prophets so called, not as though of inferior authority, but solely because of the brevity of their books. Their position in this second division of the canon is due not to the nature of their contents but to the fact that their writers were prophets in the strict and official sense. Last of all those books occupy the third place which were written by inspired men who were not in the technical or official sense prophets. Thus the writings of David and Solomon, though inspired as truly as those of the prophets, are assigned to the third division of the canon, because their authors were not prophets but kings. So, too, the book of Daniel belongs in this third division, because its author, though possessing the gift of prophecy in an eminent degree, and uttering prophecies of the most remarkable character, and hence called a prophet, Mat. xxiv. 15, in the same general sense as David is in Acts ii. 30, nevertheless did not exercise the prophetic office. He was not engaged in laboring with the people for their spiritual good as his contemporary and fellow-captive Ezekiel. He had an entirely different office to perform on their behalf in the distinguished position which he occupied at the court of Babylon and then of Persia. The books of Chronicles cover the same period of the history as 2 Samuel and Kings, but the assignment of the former to the third division, and of the latter to the second, assures us that

Samuel and Kings were written by prophets, while the author of Chronicles, though writing under the guidance and inspiration of the Holy Spirit, was not officially a prophet.

As classified in our present Hebrew Bibles, which follow the order given in the Talmud, this principle of arrangement is in one instance obviously departed from; the Lamentations of Jeremiah stands in the Hagiographa, though as the production of a prophet it ought to be included in the second division of the canon, and there is good reason to believe that this was its original position. Two modes of enumerating the sacred books were in familiar use in ancient times, as appears from the catalogues which have been preserved to us. The two books of Samuel were uniformly counted one: so the two books of Kings and the two of Chronicles: so also Ezra and Nehemiah: so likewise the Minor Prophets were counted one book. Then, according to one mode of enumeration, Ruth was attached to Judges as forming together one book, and Lamentations was regarded as a part of the book of Jeremiah: thus the entire number of the books of the Old Testament was twenty-two. In the other mode Ruth and Lamentations were reckoned separate books, and the total was twenty-four. Now the earliest enumerations that we have from Jewish or Christian sources are by Josephus [1] and Origen, who both give the number as twenty-two: and as this is the number of letters in the Hebrew alphabet, while twenty-four is the number in the Greek alphabet, the former may naturally be supposed to have been adopted by the Jews in the first instance. From this it would appear that Lamentations was originally annexed

[1] Josephus adopts a classification of his own suited to his immediate purpose, but doubtless preserves the total number current among his countrymen.

to the book of Jeremiah and of course placed in the same division of the canon. Subsequently, for liturgical or other purposes, Ruth and Lamentations were removed to the third division of the canon and included among the five small books now classed together as Megilloth or *Rolls*, which follow immediately after Psalms, Proverbs, and Job.

There are two methods by which we can proceed in investigating the organic structure of the Old Testament. We must take our departure either from the beginning or the end. These are the two points from which all the lines of progress diverge, or in which they meet in every development or growth. All that which properly belongs to it throughout its entire course is unfolded from the one and is gathered up in the other. Thus the seed may be taken, in which the whole plant is already involved in its undeveloped state, and its growth may be traced from this its initial point by observing how roots, and stem, and leaves, and flowers, and fruit proceed from it by regular progression. Or the process may be reversed and the whole be surveyed from its consummation. The plant is for the sake of the fruit; every part has its special function to perform toward its production, and the organic structure is understood when the office of each particular portion in relation to the end of the whole becomes known.

In making trial of the first of the methods just suggested, the Old Testament may be contemplated under its most obvious aspect of a course of training to which Israel was subjected for a series of ages. So regarding it there will be little difficulty in fixing upon the law of Moses as the starting-point of this grand development. God chose Israel from among the nations of the earth to be his own peculiar people, to train them up for himself by immediate communications of his will, and by manifestations of his presence and power in the midst of them. And as the first step in this process, first not only in the order of time but of rational arrangement, and the foundation of the whole, he entered into special and formal covenant with them at Sinai, and gave them a divine constitution and laws containing the undeveloped seeds and germs of all that he designed to accomplish in them and for them. The first division of the Old Testament consequently is the Pentateuch, which contains this law with its historical introduction.

The next step was to engage the people in the observance of the law thus given to them. The constitution which they had received was set in operation and allowed to work out its legitimate fruits among them and upon them. The law of God thus shaped the history of Israel: while the history added confirmation and enlargement to the law by the experience which it afforded of its workings and of the providential sanctions which attended it and by the modifications which were from time to time introduced as occasion demanded. The historical books thus constitute the second division of the Old Testament, whose office it is to record the providential application and expansion of the law.

A third step in this divine training was to have the law as originally given and as providentially expanded, wrought not only into the outward practice of the people or their national life, as shown in the historical books, but into their inward individual life and their intellectual convictions. This is the function of the poetical books, which are occupied with devout meditations or earnest reflections upon the law of God, his works and his providence, and the reproduction of the law in the heart and life. These form accordingly the third division of the Old Testament.

The law has thus been set to work upon the national

life of the people of Israel in the course of their history, and is in addition coming to be wrought more and more into their individual life and experience by devout meditation and careful reflection. But that this outward and inward development, though conducted in the one case under immediate divine superintendence, and in the other under the inspiration of the Divine Spirit, might not fail of its appointed end, there was need that this end should be held up to view and that the minds of the people should be constantly directed forward to it. With this view the prophets were raised up to reiterate, unfold, and apply the law in its true spiritual meaning, to correct abuses and misapprehensions, to recall a transgressing people to fidelity to their covenant God, and to expand to the full dimensions of the glorious future the germs and seeds of a better era which their covenant relation to Jehovah contained. They furnish thus what may be called an objective expansion of the law, and their writings form the fourth and last division of the Old Testament.

If, then, the structure of the Old Testament has been read aright, as estimated from the point of its beginning and its gradual development from that onward, it consists of four parts,[1] viz. :

1. The Pentateuch or law of Moses, the basis of the whole.

2. Its providential expansion and application to the national life in the historical books.

3. Its subjective expansion and appropriation to individual life in the poetical books.

4. Its objective expansion and enforcement in the prophetical books.

The other mode above suggested of investigating the

[1] This is substantially the same as Oehler's division first proposed in his Prolegomena zur Theologie des Alten Testaments, 1845, pp. 87-91.

structure of the Old Testament requires us to survey it
from its end, which is Christ, for whose coming and salvation it is a preparation. This brings everything into
review under a somewhat different aspect. It will yield
substantially the same division that has already been arrived at by the contrary process, and thus lends it additional confirmation, since it serves to show that this is
not a fanciful or arbitrary partition but one grounded in
the nature of the sacred volume. At the same time it is
attended with three striking and important advantages.

1. The historical, poetical, and prophetical books,
which have hitherto been considered as separate lines of
development, springing it is true from a common root,
yet pursuing each its own independent course, are by this
second method exhibited in that close relationship and
interdependence which really subsists between them, and
in their convergence to one common centre and end.

2. It makes Christ the prominent figure, and adjusts
every part of the Old Testament in its true relation to
him. He thus becomes in the classification and structural arrangement, what he is in actual fact, the end of
the whole, the controlling, forming principle of all, so that
the meaning of every part is to be estimated from its relation to him and is only then apprehended as it should
be when that relation becomes known.

3. This will give unity to the study of the entire Scriptures. Everything in the Old Testament tends to Christ
and is to be estimated from him. Everything in the
New Testament unfolds from Christ and is likewise to be
estimated from him. In fact this method pursued in other
fields will give unity and consistency to all knowledge
by making Christ the sum and centre of the whole, of
whom, and through whom, and to whom are all things.

In the first method the Old Testament was regarded
simply as a divine scheme of training. It must now be

regarded as a scheme of training directed to one definite end, the coming of Christ.

It is to be noted that the Old Testament, though preparatory for Christ and predictive of him everywhere, is not predictive of him in the same manner nor in equal measure throughout. Types and prophecies are accumulated at particular epochs in great numbers and of a striking character. And then, as if in order that these lessons might be fully learned before the attention was diverted by the impartation of others, an interval is allowed to elapse in which predictions, whether implicit or explicit, are comparatively few and unimportant. Then another brilliant epoch follows succeeded by a fresh decline; periods they may be called of activity and of repose, of instruction on the part of God followed by periods of comprehension and appropriation on the part of the people.

These periods of marked predictive character are never mere repetitions of those which preceded them. Each has its own distinctive nature and quality. It emphasizes particular aspects and gives prominence to certain characteristics of the coming Redeemer and the ultimate salvation; but others are necessarily neglected altogether or left in comparative obscurity, and if these are to be brought distinctly to view, a new period is necessary to represent them. Thus one period serves as the complement of another, and all must be combined in order to gain a complete notion of the preparation for Christ effected by the Old Testament, or of that exhibition of Messiah and his work which it was deemed requisite to make prior to his appearing.

It is further to be observed that Christ and the coming salvation are predicted negatively as well as positively. While the good things of the present point forward to the higher good in anticipation, evils endured or foretold, and imperfections in existing forms of good, suggest the blissful future by way of contrast; they awaken to a sense of wants, deficiencies, and needs which points forward to a time when they shall be supplied. The covenant relation of the people to God creates an ideal which though far from being realized as yet must some time find a complete realization. The almighty and all holy God who has made them his people will yet make them to be in character and destiny what the people of Jehovah ought to be. Now since each predictive period expresses just the resultant of the particular types and prophecies embraced within it, its character is determined by the predominant character of these types and prophecies. If these are predominantly of a negative description, the period viewed as a whole is negatively predictive. If they are prevailingly positive, they constitute a prevailingly positive period.

If now the sacred history be considered from the call of Abraham to the close of the Old Testament, it will be perceived that it spontaneously divides itself into a series of periods alternately negative and positive. There is first a period in which a want is developed in the experience of those whom God is thus training, and is brought distinctly to their consciousness. Then follows a period devoted to its supply. Then comes a new want and a fresh supply, and so on.

The patriarchal, for example, is a negative period. Its characteristic is its wants, its patient, longing expectation of a numerous seed and the possession of the land of Canaan, which are actually supplied in the time of Moses and Joshua, which is therefore the corresponding positive period.

The period of the Judges, again, possesses a negative character. The bonds which knit the nation together were too feeble and too easily dissolved. This was not the fault of their divine constitution. Had the people been faithful to their covenant God, their invisible but almighty sovereign and protector, their union would have been perfect, and as against all foreign foes they would have been invincible. But when the generation which had beheld the mighty works wrought under the leadership of Moses and Joshua had passed away, the invisible lost its hold upon a carnally minded people, and " every man did that which was right in his own eyes." They relapsed from the worship of God and obedience to his law, and were in turn forsaken by him. Hence their weakness, their civil dissensions tending to anarchy and their repeated subjugation by surrounding enemies convincing them of the need of a stronger union under a visible head, a king to go before them. This was supplied in David and Solomon, who mark the corresponding positive period.

Then follows another negative period embracing the schism, the decline of the divided kingdoms, their overthrow and the captivity, with its corresponding positive, the restoration.

If the marked and prominent features of the history now recited be regarded, and if each negative be combined with the positive which forms its appropriate complement, there will result three great predictive or preparatory periods, viz. :

1. From the call of Abraham to the death of Joshua.

2. To the death of Solomon.

3. To the close of the Old Testament.

All that precedes the call of Abraham is purely preliminary to it, and is to be classed with the first period as its introduction or explanatory antecedent.

If these divisions of the history be transferred to the Old Testament, whose structure is the subject of inquiry, it will be resolved into the following portions, viz. :

1. The Pentateuch and Joshua.

2. The recorded history as far as the death of Solomon, and the sacred writings belonging to this period. These are, principally, the Psalms of David and the Proverbs of Solomon, the great exemplars of devotional lyrics and of aphoristic or sententious verse, which gave tone and character to all the subsequent poetry of the Bible. The latter may accordingly be properly grouped with them as their legitimate expansion or appropriate complement. These echoes continue to be heard in the following period of the history, but as the keynote was struck in this, all the poetical books may be classed together here as in a sense the product of this period.

3. The rest of the historical books of the Old Testament, together with the prophetical books.

This triple division, though based on an entirely distinct principle and reached by a totally different route, is yet closely allied to the quadruple division previously made, with only divergence enough to show that the partition is not mechanical but organic, and hence no absolute severance is possible. The historical books are here partitioned relatively to the other classes of books, exhibiting a symmetrical division of three periods of divinely guided history, and at the close of each an immediate divine revelation, for which the history furnishes the preliminary training, and, in a measure, the theme. The history recorded by Moses and consummated by Joshua has as its complement the law given at Sinai and in the wilderness. The further history to the death of Solomon formed a preparation for the poetical books. The subsequent history prepares the way for the prophets, who are in like manner gathered about its concluding stages.

There is besides just difference enough between the two modes of division to reveal the unity of the whole Old Testament, and that books separated under one aspect are yet united under another. Thus Joshua, according to one method of division and one mode of conceiving of it, continues and completes the history of the Pentateuch ; the other method sees in it the opening of a new development. There is a sense, therefore, in which it is entirely legitimate to combine the Pentateuch and Joshua as together forming a Hexateuch. The promises made to the patriarchs, the exodus from Egypt, and the march through the wilderness contemplate the settlement in Canaan recorded by Joshua, and are incomplete without it. And yet in the sense in which it is currently employed by modern critics, as though the Pentateuch and the book of Joshua constituted one continuous literary production, the term Hexateuch is a misnomer. They are distinct works by distinct writers ; and the function of Joshua was quite distinct from that of Moses. Joshua, as is expressly noted at every step of his course, simply did the bidding of Moses. The book of the law was complete, and was placed in his hands at the outset as the guide of his official life. The period of legislation ended with the death of Moses ; obedience to the law already given was the requirement for the time that followed. Again the reign of Solomon may be viewed under a double aspect. It is the sequel to that of David, carrying the kingdom of Israel to a still higher pitch of prosperity and renown ; and yet in Kings it is put at the opening of a new book, since it may likewise be viewed under another aspect as containing the seeds of the dissolution that followed.

As to the general relation of these three divisions of the Old Testament there may be observed :

1. A correspondence between the first and the following divisions. The Pentateuch and Joshua fulfil their course successively in two distinct though related spheres. They contain, first, a record of individual

experience and individual training in the lives of the patriarchs; and secondly, the national experience and training of Israel under Moses and Joshua. These spheres repeat themselves, the former in the second grand division of the Old Testament, the latter in the third. The histories of the second division are predominantly the record of individual experience, and its poetry is individual in its character. Judges and Samuel are simply a series of historical biographies; Judges, of the distinguished men raised up from time to time to deliver the people out of the hands of their oppressors; Samuel, of the three leading characters by whom the affairs of the people were shaped in that important period of transition, Samuel, Saul, and David. Ruth is a biographical sketch from private life. The poetical books not only unfold the divinely guided reflections of individual minds or the inward struggles of individual souls, but their lessons, whether devotional or Messianic, are chiefly based on the personal experience of David and Solomon, or of other men of God.

The third division of the Old Testament, on the other hand, resembles the closing portion of the first in being national. Its histories—Kings, Chronicles, Ezra, and Nehemiah—concern the nation at large, and the same may be said to a certain extent even of Esther. The communications of the prophets now given are God's messages to the people, and their form and character are conditioned by the state and prospects of the nation.

2. The number of organs employed in their communication increases with each successive division. In the first there are but two inspired writers, Moses and the author of the book of Joshua, whether Joshua himself or another. In the second the historians were distinct from the poets, the latter consisting of David, Solomon, and other sacred singers, together with the author of the

book of Job. In the third we find the greatest number
of inspired writers, together with the most elaborate ar-
ticulation and hence an advance in organic structure.

3. There is a progress in the style of instruction
adopted in each successive division. The first is purely
typical. The few prophecies which are scattered
through it are lost in the general mass. The second division is of a mixed character, but types predominate.
We here meet not a simple record of typical facts and
institutions without remark or explanation, as in the
Pentateuch and Joshua; but in the poetical books types
are singled out and dwelt upon, and made the basis of
predictions respecting Christ. The third division is also
of a mixed character, but prophecies so predominate that
the types are almost lost sight of in the comparison.

4. These divisions severally render prominent the
three great theocratic offices which were combined in the
Redeemer. The first by its law, the central institution
of which is sacrifice, and which impresses a sacerdotal
organization upon the people, points to Jesus as priest.
The second, which revolves about the kingdom, is prog-
nostic of Jesus as king, although the erection of Solomon's temple and the new stability and splendor given
to the ritual show that the priesthood is not forgotten.
In the third, the prophets rise to prominence, and the
people themselves, dispersed among the nations to be the
teachers of the world, take on a prophetic character typ-
ifying Jesus as a prophet. While nevertheless the rebuilding of the temple by Zerubbabel, and the prophetic
description of its ideal reconstruction by Ezekiel, point
still to his priesthood, and the monarchs of Babylon and
Persia, aspiring to universal empire, dimly foreshadow
his kingdom.

II

THE PLAN AND CONTENTS OF THE PENTATEUCH

THE books of Moses are in the Scriptures called "the law," Josh. i. 7; "the law of Moses," 1 Kin. ii. 3; "the book of the law," Josh. viii. 34; "the book of the law of Moses," Josh. viii. 31; "the book of the law of God," Josh. xxiv. 26, or " of the LORD," 2 Chron. xvii. 9, on account of their predominantly legislative character. They are collectively called the Pentateuch, from πέντε, *five*, and τεῦχος, originally signifying an implement, but used by the Alexandrian critics in the sense of *a book*, hence a work consisting of five books. This division into five books is spoken of by Josephus and Philo, and in all probability is at least as old as the Septuagint version. Its introduction has by some (Leusden, Hävernick, Lengerke) been attributed to the Greek translators. Others regard it as of earlier date (Michaelis), and perhaps as old as the law itself (Bertholdt, Keil), for the reasons:

1. That this is a natural division determined by the plan of the work. Genesis, Leviticus, and Deuteronomy are each complete in itself; and this being so, the fivefold division follows as a matter of course.

2. The division of the Psalms into five books, as found in the Hebrew Bible, is probably patterned after the Pentateuch, and is most likely as old as the constitution of the canon.

The names of these five books are in the Hebrew Bible taken from the first words of each. Those current among ourselves, and adopted in most versions of the Old Testament, are taken from the old Greek translators.

The Pentateuch has one theme, which is consistently pursued from first to last, viz., the theocracy in Israel, or the establishment of Israel to be the people of God. It consists of two parts, viz. :

1. Historical, Gen. i.—Ex. xix., tracing the successive steps by which Israel was brought into being as a nation chosen to be the peculiar people of God.

2. Legal, recording the divine constitution granted to them, by which they were formally organized as God's people and brought into special relation to him. The law begins with the ten commandments, uttered by God's own voice from the smoking summit of Sinai, in Ex. xx., and extends to the close of Deuteronomy. The scraps of history which are found in this second main division are not only insignificant in bulk compared with the legislation which it contains, but they are subordinated to it as detailing the circumstances or occasions on which the laws were given, and likewise allied with it as constituting part of the training by which Israel was schooled into their proper relation to God. Of these two main sections of the Pentateuch the first, or historical portion, is not only precedent to, but preparatory for, the second or legal portion ; the production and segregation of the people of Israel being effected with the direct view of their being organized as the people of God.

It will be plain from a general survey of these two main sections, into which the Pentateuch is divided, that everything in it bears directly upon its theme as already stated ; and the more minute and detailed the examination of its contents, the more evident this will become. The first of these two great sections, or the historical portion, is clearly subdivided by the call of Abraham. It was at that point that the production and segregation of the covenant people, strictly speaking, commenced. From the creation of the world to the call of Abraham, which is embraced in the first eleven chapters of Gene-sis, the history is purely preliminary. It is directed to the negative end of demonstrating the necessity of such a segregation. From the call of Abraham to the law given at Mount Sinai, that is to say, from Gen. xii. to Ex. xix., the history is directed to the positive end of the production and segregation of the covenant people.

The preliminary portion of the history is once more divided by the flood ; the first five chapters of Genesis being occupied with the antediluvian period and the next six with an account of the deluge and the postdiluvian period. Each of these preliminary periods is marked by the formation of a universal covenant between God and the two successive progenitors and heads of the hu-man race, Adam and Noah, which stand in marked con-trast with the particular or limited covenant made with Abraham, the progenitor of the chosen race, at the begin-ning of the following or patriarchal period. The failure of both those primeval covenants to preserve religion among men, and to guard the race from degeneracy and open apostasy, established the necessity of a new ex-pedient, the segregation of a chosen race, among whom religion might be fostered in seclusion from other na-tions, until it could gain strength enough to contend with evil on the arena of the world and overcome it, in-stead of being overcome by it. The covenant with Adam was broken by his fall, and the race became more and more corrupt from age to age, until the LORD determined to put a sudden end to its enormous wickedness, and de-stroyed the world by the flood. Noah, who was alone spared with his household, became the head of a new race with whom God entered into covenant afresh ; but the impious attempt at Babel is suggestive of the ungod-liness and corruption which once more overspread the earth, and it became apparent, if the true service of God was to be maintained in the world, it must be by initiating a new process. Hence the call of Abraham to be the father of a new people, which should be kept separate from other nations and be the peculiar people of the LORD.

These two preliminary periods furnish thus the justification of the theocracy in Israel by demonstrating the insufficiency of preceding methods, and the consequent necessity of selecting a special people to be the LORD's people. But besides this negative purpose, which the writer had in view in recording this primeval portion of the history, he had also the positive design of paving the way for the account to be subsequently given of the chosen people, by exhibiting and inculcating certain ideas, which are involved in the notion of a covenant people, and of describing certain preliminary steps already taken in the direction of selecting such a people.

The idea of the people of God involves, when contemplated under its negative aspect, (1) segregation from the rest of mankind ; and this segregation is not purely formal and local, but is represented (2) both in their inward character, suggesting the contrast of holiness to sin, and (3) in their outward destiny, suggesting the contrast of salvation to perdition. The same idea of the people of God contemplated under its positive aspect involves (4) direct relation to God or covenant with him, the observance of his laws and of the institutions which he imposed or established. Something is effected in relation to each of these four particulars in each of these preliminary periods, and thus much, at least, accomplished in the direction of the theocracy which was afterward to be instituted.

Genesis begins with a narrative of the creation, because in this the sacred history has its root. And this not only because an account of the formation of the world might fitly precede an account of what was transacted in it, but chiefly because the sacred history is essentially a history of redemption, and this being a process of recovery, a scheme initiated for the purpose of restoring man and the world to their original condition, necessarily presupposes a knowledge of what that original condition was. Hence the regular and emphatic repetition, after each work was performed, in Gen. i., of the statement, " and God saw that it was good;" and at the close of all, " God saw everything that he had made; and behold it was very good." Hence, too, the declaration made and repeated at the creation of man, that he was made in God's image. The idea of primitive holiness thus set forth is further illustrated, by contrast, in the tree of the knowledge of good and evil, which stood in the midst of the garden, and was made the test of obedience, and especially in man's transgression and disobedience which rendered redemption necessary. The contrast of salvation and perdition is suggested by paradise and the tree of life on the one hand, and by the curse pronounced upon man and his expulsion from Eden in consequence of the fall upon the other; by Cain's being driven out from the presence of the LORD, and by Enoch, who walked with God and was not, for God took him. The idea of segregation is suggested by the promise respecting the seed of the woman and the seed of the serpent, by which the family of man is divided into two opposite and hostile classes, who maintain a perpetual strife, until the serpent and his seed are finally crushed; a strife which culminates in the personal conflict between Christ and Satan, and the victory of the former, in which all his people share. These hostile parties find their first representatives in the family of Adam himself—in Cain, who was of the evil one, and his righteous brother, Abel; and after Abel's murder Seth was raised up in his stead. These

are perpetuated in their descendants, those of Seth being
called the sons of God, those of Cain the sons and
daughters of men. In conformity with the plan, which
the writer steadfastly pursues throughout, of tracing the
divergent lines of descent before dismissing them from
further consideration in the history, and proceeding with
the account of the chosen line itself, he first gives an account of the descendants of Cain, whose growing degeneracy is exhibited in Lamech, of the seventh generation
(Gen. iv. 17–24), before narrating the birth of Seth (Gen.
iv. 25, 26) and tracing the line of the pious race through
him to Noah, ch. v. By this excision of the apostate line
of Cain, that narrowing process is begun, which was finally
to issue in the limitation to Abraham and his seed. And
in the fourth and last place, the divine institutions now
established as germs of the future law, were the weekly
Sabbath (Gen. ii. 3), and the rite of sacrifice (Gen. iv. 3, 4).

In the next period the same rites were perpetuated,
with a more specific mention of the distinction of clean
and unclean animals (Gen. vii. 8), and the prohibition
of eating blood (Gen. ix. 4), which were already involved
in the institution of sacrifice, and the annexing of the
penalty of death to the crime of murder (Gen. ix. 6); and
the same ideas received a new sanction and enforcement.
The character of those who belong to God is represented in righteous Noah, as contrasted with the ungodly world; their destiny, in the salvation of the former
and the perdition of the latter. Segregation is carried
one term farther by the promise belonging to this period,
which declares that while Japheth shall be enlarged and
Canaan made a servant, God shall dwell in the tents
of Shem. And here, according to his usual method, already adverted to, the writer first presents a view of the
descendants of all Noah's sons, which were dispersed
over the face of the earth (Gen. x.), prior to tracing the

chosen line in the seed of Shem, to Terah, the father of Abraham (Gen. xi. 10–26). He thus exhibits the relationship of the chosen race to the rest of mankind, while singling them out and sundering them from it. Everything in these opening chapters thus bears directly on his grand theme, to which he at once proceeds by stating the call of Abraham (Gen. xii.), and going on to trace those providential events which issued in the production of a great nation descended from him.

The preparation of the people of Israel, who were to be made the covenant people of God, is traced in two successive stages : first, the family, in the remainder of the book of Genesis (Gen. ch. xii.–l.), secondly, the nation (Ex. i.–xix.).

The first of these sections embraces the histories of the patriarchs, Abraham, Isaac, and Jacob. God made choice of Abraham to be the father of his own peculiar people, and covenanted with him as well as with Isaac and Jacob severally to be their God, promising to them— (1) a numerous seed, (2) the possession of the land of Canaan, and (3) that a blessing should come through them upon all mankind. During this period the work of segregation and elimination previously begun was carried steadily forward to its final term. The line had already been narrowed down to the family of Terah in the preceding chapter. Abraham is now called to leave his father's house (Gen. xii.), his nephew Lot accompanying him, who is soon, however, separated from him (ch. xiii.), and his descendants traced (xix. 37, 38). Then in Abraham's own family Ishmael is sent away from his house (ch. xxi.), and the divergent lines of descent from Keturah and from Ishmael are traced (ch. xxv.), before proceeding with the direct line through Isaac (xxv. 19). Then in Isaac's family the divergent line of Esau is traced (ch. xxxvi.), before proceeding with the direct line of Jacob (xxxvii. 2), the father of the twelve tribes, after which no further elimination is necessary.

The history of this sacred family and God's gracious leadings in Canaan are first detailed, and then the providential steps are recorded by which they were taken down into Egypt, where they were to be unfolded to a great nation. One important stage of preparation for the theocracy in Israel is now finished : the family period is at an end, the national period is about to begin. Genesis here accordingly breaks off with the death of Jacob and of Joseph.

Exodus opens with a succinct statement of the immense and rapid multiplication of the children of Israel, effecting the transition from a family to a nation (Ex. i. 1–7), and then proceeds at once to detail the preparations for the exodus (i. 8–ch. xiii.), and the exodus itself (ch. xiv.–xix.). There is first described the negative preparation in the hard bondage imposed on the people by the king of Egypt, making them sigh for deliverance (i. 8–22). The positive preparation follows, first of an instrument to lead the people out of Egypt in the person of Moses (ch. ii.–vi.) ; second, the breaking their bonds and setting them free by the plagues sent on Egypt (ch. vii.–xiii). The way being thus prepared, the people are led out of Egypt, attended by marvellous displays of God's power and grace, which conducted them through the Red Sea and attended them on their march to Sinai (ch. xiv.–xix.).

Israel is now ready to be organized as the people of God. The history is accordingly succeeded by the legislation of the Pentateuch. This legislation consists of three parts, corresponding to three periods of very unequal length into which the abode in the wilderness may be divided, and three distinct localities severally occupied by the people in these periods respectively.

1. The legislation at Mount Sinai during the year that they encamped there.

2. That given in the period of wandering in the wilderness of Paran, which occupied the greater part of the forty years.

3. That given to Israel in the plains of Moab, on the east of Jordan, when they had almost reached the promised land.

At Sinai God first proclaims the law of the ten commandments (Ex. xx.), and then gives a series of ordinances (ch. xxi.–xxiii.) as the basis of his covenant with Israel, which is then formally ratified (ch. xxiv.). The way is thus prepared for God to take up his abode in Israel. Accordingly directions are at once given for the preparation of the tabernacle as God's dwelling-place, with its furniture, and for the appointment of priests to serve in it, with a description of the vestments which they should wear, and the rites by which they should be consecrated (ch. xxv.–xxxi.). The execution of these directions was postponed in consequence of the breach of the covenant by the sin of the golden calf and the renewal of the covenant which this had rendered necessary (ch. xxxii.–xxxiv.). And then Exodus is brought to a termination by the account of the actual construction and setting up of the tabernacle and God's taking up his abode in it (ch. xxxv.–xl.).

The LORD having thus formally entered into covenant with Israel, and fixed his residence in the midst of them, next gives them his laws. These are mainly contained in the book of Leviticus. There is first the law respecting the various kinds of sacrifices to be offered at the tabernacle now erected (Lev. i.–vii.), then the consecration of Aaron and his sons by whom they were to be offered, together with the criminal conduct and death of two of his sons, Nadab and Abihu (ch. viii.–x.) ; then the law respecting clean and unclean meats and various kinds of purifications (ch. xi.–xv.), and the series is wound up by the services of the day of atonement, effecting the highest expiation known to the Mosaic ritual (ch. xvi.). These are followed by ordinances of a more miscellaneous character relating to the people (ch. xvii.–xx.), and the priests (ch. xxi., xxii.), the various festivals (ch. xxiii.), the sabbatical year and year of jubilee (ch. xxv.); and the whole is concluded by the blessing pronounced on obedience and the curse which would attend upon transgression (ch. xxvi.), with which the book is brought to a formal close (xxvi. 46). A supplementary chapter (xxvii.) is added at the end respecting vows.

Numbers begins with the arrangements of the camp and preparations for departure from Sinai (Num. i.–x.). The people are numbered (ch. i.), the order of encampment and march settled (ch. ii.), and duties assigned to the several families of the Levites in transporting the tabernacle (ch. iii., iv.). Then, after some special ceremonial regulations (ch. v., vi.), follow the offerings at the dedication of the tabernacle, including oxen and wagons for its transportation (ch. vii.); the Levites are consecrated for their appointed work (ch. viii.), and as the final act before removal the passover was celebrated (ch. ix.), and signal trumpets prepared (ch. x.). Then comes the actual march from Sinai, with the occurrences upon the journey to Kadesh, on the southern border of the land, where they are condemned to wander forty years in the wilderness on account of the rebellious refusal to enter Canaan (ch. xi.–xiv.). Some incidents belonging to the period of the wandering and laws then given are recorded (ch. xv.–xix.). The assembling of the people again at Kadesh in the first month of the fortieth year, the sin of Moses and Aaron, which excluded them from the promised land, and the march to the plains of Moab, opposite Jericho, with the transactions there until the eleventh month of that year, including the conquest of the territory east of the Jordan occupy the remainder of the book (ch. xx.–xxxvi.).

Deuteronomy contains the last addresses of Moses to the people in the plains of Moab, delivered in the eleventh month of the fortieth year of Israel's wanderings, in which he endeavors to engage them to the faithful observance of the law now given. The first of these addresses (Deut. i.–iv. 40) reviews some of the leading events of the march through the wilderness as arguments for a steadfast adherence to the LORD's service. Then after selecting three cities of refuge on the east side of the Jordan (iv. 41–43), he proceeds in his second address with a declaration of the law, first in general terms, reciting the ten commandments with earnest admonitions of fidelity to the LORD (ch. v.–xi.), then entering more into detail in the inculcation of the various ordinances and enactments (ch. xii.–xxvi.). This law of Deuteronomy thus set before the people for their guidance is properly denominated the people's code as distinguished from the ritual law in Exodus, Leviticus, and Numbers, which is denominated the priests' code, being intended particularly for the guidance of the priests in all matters connected with the ceremonial. The latter develops in detail under symbolic forms the privileges and duties springing out of the covenant relation of the people to Jehovah in their access to him and the services of his worship. The former is a development of the covenant code (Ex. xx.–xxiii.), with such modifications as were suggested by the experience of the last forty years, and especially by their approaching entrance into the land of Canaan. His third address sets solemnly before the people in two sections (ch. xxvii., xxviii., and ch. xxix., xxx.), the blessing consequent upon obedience and the curse that will certainly follow transgression.

Provision is then made both for the publication and

safe-keeping of the law, by delivering it to the custody of the priests, who are directed to publish it in the audience of the people every seven years, and to keep it safely in the side of the ark (ch. xxxi.); next follow Moses's admonitory song (ch. xxxii.), his last blessing to the tribes (ch. xxxiii.), and his death (ch. xxxiv.).

The Pentateuch accordingly has, as appears from this brief survey, one theme from first to last to which all that it contains relates. This is throughout treated upon one definite plan, which is steadfastly adhered to. And it contains a continuous, unbroken history from the creation to the death of Moses, without any chasms or interruptions. The only chasms which have been alleged are merely apparent, not real, and grow out of the nature of the theme and the rigor with which it is adhered to. It has been said that while the lives of the patriarchs are given in minute detail a large portion of the four hundred and thirty years during which the children of Israel dwelt in Egypt is passed over in silence; and that of a large part of the forty years' wandering in the wilderness nothing is recorded. But the fact is, that these offered little that fell within the plan of the writer. The long residence in Egypt contributed nothing to the establishment of the theocracy in Israel, but the development of the chosen seed from a family to a nation. This is stated in a few verses, and it is all that it was necessary to record. So with the period of judicial abandonment in the wilderness: it was not the purpose of the writer to relate everything that happened, but only what contributed to the establishment of God's kingdom in Israel; and the chief fact of importance was the dying out of the old generation and the growing up of a new one in their stead.

The unity of theme and unity of plan now exhibited creates a presumption that these books are, as they have been traditionally believed to be, the product of a single writer; and the presumption thus afforded must stand unless satisfactory proof can be brought to the contrary.

SCHEME OF THE PENTATEUCH.

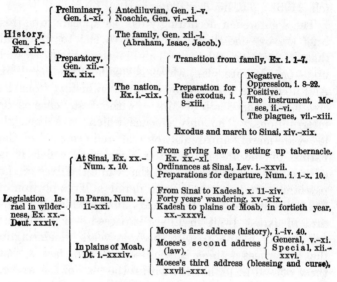

Conclusion, xxxi.–xxxiv.

III

MOSES THE AUTHOR OF THE PENTATEUCH

IF the Pentateuch is what it claims to be, it is of the greatest interest and value. It professes to record the origin of the world and of the human race, a primitive state of innocence from which man fell by yielding to temptation, the history of the earliest ages, the relationship subsisting between the different nations of mankind, and particularly the selection of Abraham and his descendants to be the chosen people of God, the depositaries of divine revelation, in whose line the Son of God should in due time become incarnate as the Saviour of the world. It further contains an account of the providential events accompanying the development of the seed of Abraham from a family to a nation, their exodus from Egypt, and the civil and religious institutions under which they were organized in the prospect of their entry into, and occupation of, the land of Canaan. The contents of the Pentateuch stand thus in intimate relation to the problems of physical and ethnological science, to history and archæology and religious faith. All the subsequent revelations of the Bible, and the gospel of Jesus Christ itself, rest upon the foundation of what is contained in the Pentateuch, as they either presuppose or directly affirm its truth.

It is a question of primary importance, therefore, both in itself and in its consequences, whether the Pentateuch is a veritable, trustworthy record, or is a heterogeneous mass of legend and fable from which only a modicum of truth can be doubtfully and with difficulty elicited. Can we lay it at the basis of our investigations, and implicitly trust its representations, or must we admit that its unsupported word can only be received with caution, and that of itself it carries but little weight? In the settlement of this matter a consideration of no small consequence is that of the authorship of the Pentateuch. Its credibility is, of course, not absolutely dependent upon its Mosaic authorship. It might be all true, though it were written by another than Moses and after his time. But if it was written by Moses, then the history of the Mosaic age was recorded by a contemporary and eyewitness, one who was himself a participant and a leader in the scenes which he relates, and the legislator from whom the enactments proceeded ; and it must be confessed that there is in this fact the highest possible guaranty of the accuracy and truthfulness of the whole. It is to the discussion of this point that the present chapter is devoted : Is the Pentateuch the work of Moses?

1. It is universally conceded that this was the traditional opinion among the Jews. To this the New Testament bears the most abundant and explicit testimony. The Pentateuch is by our Lord called "the book of Moses" (Mark xii. 26) ; when it is read and preached the apostles say that Moses is read (2 Cor. iii. 15) and preached (Acts xv. 21). The Pentateuch and the books of the prophets, which were read in the worship of the synagogue, are called both by our Lord (Luke xvi. 29, 31) and the evangelists (Luke xxiv. 27), "Moses and the prophets," or "the law of Moses and the prophets" (Luke xxiv. 44 ; Acts xxviii. 23). Of the injunctions of the Pentateuch not only do the Jews say, when addressing our Lord, "Moses commanded" (John viii. 5), but our Lord repeatedly uses the same form of speech (Mat. viii. 4; xix. 7, 8; Mark i. 44; x. 3; Luke v. 14), as testified by three of the evangelists. Of the law in general

he says, "Moses gave the law" (John vii. 19), and the
evangelist echoes "the law was given by Moses" (John
i. 17). And that Moses was not only the author of the
law, but committed its precepts to writing, is affirmed by
the Jews (Mark xii. 19), and also by our Lord (Mark x.
5), who further speaks of him as writing predictions respecting himself (John v. 46, 47), and also traces a narrative in the Pentateuchal history to him (Mark xii. 26).

It has been said that our Lord here speaks not authoritatively but by accommodation to the prevailing sentiment of the Jews; and that it was not his purpose to
settle questions in Biblical Criticism. But the fact remains that he, in varied forms of speech, explicitly con-
firms the current belief that Moses wrote the books
ascribed to him. For those who reverently accept him
as an infallible teacher this settles the question. The
only alternative is to assume that he was not above the
liability to err; in other words, to adopt what has been
called the kenotic view of his sacred person, that he completely emptied himself of his divine nature in his incar-
nation, and during his abode on earth was subject to all
the limitations of ordinary men. Such a lowering of
view respecting the incarnate person of our Lord may
logically affect the acceptance of his instructions in other
matters. He himself says (John iii. 12), "If I have
told you earthly things and ye believe not, how shall ye
believe if I tell you of heavenly things?"

2. That the Pentateuch was the production of Moses,
and the laws which it contains were the laws of Moses,
was the firm faith of Israel from the beginning, and is
clearly reflected in every part of the Old Testament, as
we have already seen to be the case in the New Testament. The final injunction of the last of the prophets
(Mal. iv. 4) is, "Remember ye the law of Moses my servant, which I commanded unto him in Horeb for all Is-

3

rael, with the statutes and judgments." The regulations adopted by the Jews returned from captivity were not recent enactments of their leaders, but the old Mosaic institutions restored. Thus (Ezra iii. 2) they built the altar and established the ritual "as it is written in the law of Moses." After the new temple was finished they set priests and Levites to their respective service, " as it is written in the book of Moses " (Ezra vi. 18). When subsequently Ezra led up a fresh colony from Babylon, he is characterized as " a ready scribe in the law of Moses " (Ezra vii. 6). At a formal assembly of the people held for the purpose, " the book of the law of Moses " was read and explained to them day by day (Neh. viii. 1, 18). Allusions are made to the injunctions of the Pentateuch in general or in particular as the law which God gave to Moses (Neh. i. 7, 8 ; viii. 14 ; ix. 14 ; x. 29), as written in the law (vs. 34, 36), or contained in the book of Moses (Neh. xiii. 1).

In the Captivity Daniel (ix. 11, 13) refers to matters contained in the Pentateuch as "written in the law of Moses." After the long defection of Manasseh and Amon, the neglected "book of the law of the LORD by Moses " (2 Kin. xxii. 8 ; xxiii. 25 ; 2 Chron. xxxiv. 14 ; xxxv. 6, 12) was found in the temple, and the reformation of Josiah was in obedience to its instructions. The passover of Hezekiah was observed according to the prescriptions of " the law of Moses " (2 Chron. xxx. 16), and in general Hezekiah is commended for having kept the " commandments which the LORD commanded Moses " (2 Kin. xviii. 6). The ten tribes were carried away captive because they "transgressed " what " Moses commanded " (2 Kin. xviii. 12) ; king Amaziah did (2 Kin. xiv. 6 ; 2 Chron. xxv. 4) " as it is written in the book of the law of Moses," Deut. xxiv. 16 being here quoted in exact terms. The high-priest Jehoiada directed the ritual " as it is written in the law of Moses" (2 Chron. xxiii. 18), while appointing the singing as it was ordained by David ; a discrimination which shows that there was no such legal fiction, as it has sometimes been contended, by which laws in general, even though recent, were attributed to Moses. David charged Solomon (1 Kin. ii. 3 ; 1 Chron. xxii. 13) to keep what " is written in the law of Moses," and a like charge was addressed by the LORD to David himself (2 Kin. xxi. 7, 8 ; 2 Chron. xxxiii. 8). Solomon appointed the ritual in his temple in accordance with " the commandment of Moses " (2 Chron. viii. 13 ; 1 Chron. vi. 49). When the ark was taken by David to Zion, it was borne " as Moses commanded " (1 Chron. xv. 15; cf. 2 Sam. vi. 13). Certain of the Canaanites were left in the land in the time of Joshua, " to prove Israel by them, to know whether they would hearken unto the commandments of the LORD, which he commanded their fathers by the hand of Moses " (Judg. iii. 4). Joshua was directed " to do according to all the law which Moses commanded," and was told that " the book of the law should not depart out of his mouth " (Josh. i. 7, 8). And in repeated instances it is noted with what exactness he followed the directions given by Moses.

It is to be presumed, at least until the contrary is shown, that " the law " and " the book of the law " have the same sense throughout as in the New Testament, as also in Josephus and in the prologue to the book of Sirach or Ecclesiasticus, where they are undeniably identical with the Pentateuch. The testimonies which have been reviewed show that this was from the first attributed to Moses. At the least it is plain that the sacred historians of the Old Testament, without exception, knew of a body of laws which were universally obligatory and were believed to be the laws of Moses, and which answer in every particular to the laws of the Pentateuch.

3. Let us next inquire what the Pentateuch says of itself. It may be roughly divided for our present purpose into its two main sections: (1) Genesis and Exodus (i.–xix.), historical; (2) Ex. xx.–Deuteronomy, mainly legal. The legal portion consists of three distinct bodies of law, each of which has its own peculiar character and occasion. The first is denominated the Book of the Covenant and embraces Ex. xx.–xxiii., the ten commandments with the accompanying judgments or ordinances, which were the stipulations of the covenant then formally ratified between the LORD and the people. This Moses is expressly said (Ex. xxiv. 4), to have written and read in the audience of the people, who promised obedience, whereupon the covenant was concluded with appropriate sacrificial rites.

By this solemn transaction Israel became the LORD's covenant people, and he in consequence established his dwelling in the midst of them and there received their worship. This gave occasion to the second body of laws, the so-called Priest Code, relating to the sanctuary and the ritual. This is contained in the rest of Exodus (xxv.–xl.), with the exception of three chapters (xxxii.–xxxiv.) relating to the sin of the golden calf, the whole of Leviticus, and the regulations found in the book of Numbers, where they are intermingled with the history, which suggests the occasion of the laws and supplies the connecting links. This Priest Code is expressly declared in all its parts to have been directly communicated by the LORD to Moses, in part on the summit of Mount Sinai during his forty days' abode there, in part while Israel lay encamped at the base of the mountain, and in part during their subsequent wanderings in the wilderness.

The third body of law is known as the Deuteronomic Code, and embraces the legal portion of the book of Deuteronomy, which was delivered by Moses to the people in the plains of Moab, in immediate prospect of Canaan, in the eleventh month of the fortieth year of their wanderings in the wilderness. This Moses is expressly said to have written and to have committed to the custody of the Levites, who bore the ark of the covenant (Deut. xxxi. 9, 24–26).[1]

The entire law, therefore, in explicit and positive terms, claims to be Mosaic. The book of the Covenant and the Deuteronomic law are expressly affirmed to have been written by Moses. The Priest Code, or the ritual law, was given by the LORD to Moses, and by him to Aaron and his sons, though Moses is not in so many words said to have written it.

Turning now from the laws of the Pentateuch to its narratives we find two passages expressly attributed to the pen of Moses. After the victory over Amalek at Rephidim, the LORD said unto Moses (Ex. xvii. 14), "Write this for a memorial in a book." The fact that

[1] "This law," the words of which Moses is said to have written in a book until they were finished, cannot be restricted with Robertson Smith to Deut. xii.–xxvi., as is evident from iv. 44, nor even with Dillmann to v.–xxvi., as appears from i. 5 ; xxviii. 58, 61; xxix. 20, 27. It is doubtful whether it can even be limited to Deut. i.–xxxi. In favor of the old opinion, that it embraced in addition the preceding books of the Pentateuch, may be urged that Deuteronomy itself recognizes a prior legislation of Moses binding upon Israel (iv. 5, 14 ; xxix. 1; xvii. 9–11; xxiv. 8 ; xxvii. 26, which affirms as " words of this law " the antecedent curses (vs. 15–25), some of which are based on laws peculiar to Leviticus); and the book of the law of Moses, by which Joshua was guided (Josh. i. 7, 8), must have been quite extensive. Comp. Josh. i. 3–5a, and Deut. xi. 24, 25 ; Josh. i. 5b, 6, and Deut. xxxi. 6, 7; Josh. i. 12–15, and Num. xxxii. ; Josh. v. 2–8, and Ex. xii. 48; Josh. v. 10, 11, and Lev. xxiii. 5, 7, 11, 14; Josh. viii. 30, 31, and Deut. xxvii ; Josh. viii. 34, and Deut. xxviii. ; Josh. xiv. 1–3a, and Num. xxxiv. 13–18 ; Josh. xiv. 6–14, and Num. xiv. 24 ; Josh. xvii. 3, 4, and Num. xxvii. 6, 7 ; Josh. xx., and Num. xxxv. 10 sqq. ; Josh. xx. 7, and Deut. iv. 43; Josh. xxi., and Num. xxxv. 1–8; Josh. xxii. 1–4, and Num. xxxii.; Josh. xxii. 5, and Deut. x. 12, 13.

such an injunction was given to Moses in this particular instance seems to imply that he was the proper person to place on record whatever was memorable and worthy of preservation in the events of the time. And it may perhaps be involved in the language used that Moses had already begun, or at least contemplated, the preparation of a connected narrative, to which reference is here made, since in the original the direction is not as in the English version, " write in *a* book," but " in *the* book." No stress is here laid, however, upon this form of expression for two reasons : (1) The article is indicated not by the letters of the text, but by the Massoretic points, which though in all probability correct, are not the immediate work of the sacred writer. (2) The article may, as in Num. v. 23, simply denote the book which would be required for writing.

Again, in Num. xxxiii. 2, a list of the various stations of the children of Israel in their marches or their wanderings in the wilderness is ascribed to Moses, who is said to have written their goings out according to their journeys by the commandment of the LORD.

This is the more remarkable and important, because this list is irreconcilable with any of the divisive theories which undertake to parcel the text of the Pentateuch among different writers. It traverses all the so-called documents, and is incapable of being referred to any one; and no assumptions of interpolations or of manipulation by the redactor can relieve the embarrassment into which the advocates of critical partition are thrown by this chapter. There is no escape from the conclusion that the author of this list of stations was the author of the entire Pentateuchal narrative from the departure out of Egypt to the arrival at the plains of Moab. [1]

[1] See Hebraica viii., pp. 237-239 ; Presbyterian and Reformed Review, April, 1894, pp., 281-284.

No explicit statements are made in the Pentateuch itself in regard to any other paragraphs of the history than these two.   But it is obvious from the whole plan and constitution of the Pentateuch that the history and the legislation are alike integral parts of one complete work. Genesis and the opening chapters of Exodus are plainly preliminary to the legislation that follows.   The historical chapters of Numbers constitute the framework in which the laws are set, binding them all together and exhibiting the occasion of each separate enactment.   If the legislation in its present form is, as it claims to be, Mosaic, then beyond all controversy the preparatory and connecting history must be Mosaic likewise.   If the laws, as we now have them, came from Moses, by inevitable sequence the history was shaped by the same hand, and the entire Pentateuch, history as well as legislation, must be what it has already been seen all after ages steadfastly regarded it, the production of Moses.

4. The style in which the laws of the Pentateuch are framed, and the terms in which they are drawn up, correspond with the claim which they make for themselves, and which all subsequent ages make for them, that they are of Mosaic origin.   Their language points unmistakably to the sojourn in the wilderness prior to the occupation of Canaan as the time when they were produced. The people are forbidden alike to do after the doings of the land of Egypt, wherein they had dwelt, or those of the land of Canaan, whither God was bringing them (Lev. xviii. 3).   They are reminded (Deut. xii. 9) that they had not yet come to the rest and the inheritance which the LORD their God was giving them.   The standing designation of Canaan is the land which the LORD giveth thee to possess it (Deut. xv. 4, 7).   The laws look forward to the time " when thou art come into the land, etc., and

shalt possess it" (Deut. xvii. 14 ; Lev. xiv. 34, etc.) ; or
" when the LORD hath cut off these nations and thou suc-
ceedest them, and dwellest in their cities " (Deut. xix. 1),
as the period when they are to go into full operation
(Deut. xii. 1, 8, 9). The place of sacrifice is not where
Jehovah has fixed his habitation, but " the place which
Jehovah shall choose to place his name there " (Deut.
xii. 5, etc.). Israel is contemplated as occupying a camp
(Num. v. 2–4, etc.) and living in tents (Lev. xiv. 8), and
in the wilderness (Lev. xvi. 21, 22). The bullock of the
sin-offering was to be burned without the camp (Lev. iv.
12, 21) ; the ashes from the altar were to be carried
without the camp (vi. 11). The leper was to have his
habitation without the camp (xiii. 46) ; the priest was to
go forth out of the camp to inspect him (xiv. 3) ; ceremonies are prescribed for his admission to the camp
(ver. 8) as well as the interval which must elapse before
his return to his own tent. In slaying an animal for
food, the only possibilities suggested are that it may be
in the camp or out of the camp (xvii. 3). The law of
the consecration of priests respects by name Aaron and
his sons (viii. 2 sqq.). Two of these sons, Nadab and Abihu, commit an offence which causes their death, a circumstance which calls forth some special regulations
(Lev. ch. x.), among others those of the annual day of
atonement (Lev. xvi. 1) on which Aaron was the cele-
brant (ver. 3 sqq.), and the camp and the wilderness the
locality (vs. 21, 22, 26, 27). The tabernacle, the ark, and
other sacred vessels were made of shittim wood (Ex.
xxxvi. 20), which was peculiar to the wilderness. The
sacred structure was made of separate boards, so joined
together that it could be readily taken apart, and explicit
directions are given for its transportation as Israel journeyed from place to place (Num. iv. 5 sqq.), and gifts of
wagons and oxen were made for the purpose (Num.

vii.). Specific instructions are given for the arrangement
of the several tribes, both in their encampments and their
marches (Num. ii.). Silver trumpets were made to direct
the calling of the assembly and the journeying of the
host (Num. x. 2 sqq.). The ceremonies of the red heifer
were to be performed without the camp (Num. xix. 3, 7,
9) and by Eleazar personally (vs. 3, 4). The law of puri-
fication provides simply for death in tents and in the
open fields (vs. 14, 16).

The peculiarity of these laws carries with it the evidence that they were not only enacted during the sojourn in the wilderness, but that they were then committed to writing. Had they been preserved orally, the
forms of expression would have been changed insensibly,
to adapt them to the circumstances of later times. It is
only the unvarying permanence of a written code, that
could have perpetuated these laws in a form which in
after ages, when the people were settled in Canaan, and
Aaron and his sons were dead, no longer described directly and precisely the thing to be done, but must be
mentally adapted to an altered state of affairs before they
could be carried into effect.

The laws of Deuteronomy are, besides, prefaced by two
farewell addresses delivered by Moses to Israel on the
plains of Moab (Deut. i. 5 sqq. ; v. 1 sqq.), which are precisely adapted to the situation, and express those feel-
ings to which the great leader might most appropriately
have given utterance under the circumstances. And the
most careful scrutiny shows that the diction and style of
thought in these addresses is identical with that of the
laws that follow. Both have emanated from one mind
and pen. The laws of Deuteronomy are further followed
by a prophetic song (Deut. xxxii.) which Moses is said
to have written (xxxi. 22), and by a series of blessings upon
the several tribes, which he is said to have pronounced

before his death (xxxiii. 1), all which are entirely appropriate in the situation.

The genuineness of these laws is further vouched for by the consideration that a forged body of statutes could never be successfully imposed upon any people. These laws entered minutely into the affairs of daily life, imposed burdens that would not have been voluntarily assumed, and could only have been exacted by competent authority. That they were submitted to and obeyed, is evidence that they really were ordained by Moses, in whose name they were issued. If they had first made their appearance in a later age, the fraud would inevitably have been detected. The people could not have been persuaded that enactments, never before heard of, had come down from the great legislator, and were invested with his authority.

And the circumstance that these laws are said to have been given at Mount Sinai, in the wilderness, or in the plains of Moab, is also significant. How came they to be attributed to a district outside of the holy land, which had no sacred associations in the present or in the patriarchal age, unless they really were enacted there? and if so, this could only have been in the days of Moses.

5. The Pentateuch is either directly alluded to, or its existence implied in numerous passages in the subsequent books of the Bible. The book of Joshua, which records the history immediately succeeding the age of Moses, is full of these allusions. It opens with the children of Israel in the plains of Moab, and on the point of crossing the Jordan, just where Deuteronomy left them. The arrangements for the conquest and the subsequent division of the land are in precise accordance with the directions of Moses, and are executed in professed obedience to his orders. The relationship is so pervading, and the correspondence so exact that those who dispute

the genuineness and authenticity of the Pentateuch are obliged to deny that of Joshua likewise. The testimony rendered to the existence of the Pentateuch by the books of Chronicles at every period of the history which they cover, is so explicit and repeated that it can only be set aside by impugning the truth of their statements and alleging that the writer has throughout colored the facts which he reports by his own prepossessions, and has substituted his own imagination, or the mistaken belief of a later period, for the real state of the case.

But the evidence furnished by the remaining historical books, though less abundant and clear, tends in the same direction. And it is the same with the books of the prophets and the Psalms. We find scattered everywhere allusions to the facts recorded in the Pentateuch, to its institutions, and sometimes to its very language, which afford cumulative proof that its existence was known, and its standard authority recognized by the writers of all the books subsequent to the Mosaic age. (See note 1, p. 52.)

6. Separate mention should here be made, and stress laid upon the fact, which is abundantly attested, that the Pentateuch was known, and its authority admitted in the apostate kingdom of the ten tribes from the time of the schism of Jeroboam. In order to perpetuate his power and prevent the return of the northern tribes to the sway of the house of David, he established a separate sanctuary and set up an idolatrous worship. Both the rulers and the people had the strongest inducement to disown the Pentateuch, by which both their idolatrous worship and their separate national existence were so severely condemned. And yet the evidence is varied and abundant that their national life, in spite of its degeneracy, had not wholly emancipated itself from the institutions of the Pentateuch, and that even their debased worship

was but a perverted form of that purer service which the laws of Moses had ordained.

It was at one time thought that the Samaritan Pentateuch supplied a strong argument at this point. The Samaritans, while they recognized no other portion of the canon of the Old Testament, are in possession of the Pentateuch in the Hebrew language, but written in a peculiar character, which is a more ancient and primitive form of the alphabet than that which is found in any Hebrew manuscript. It was argued, that such was the hostility between Jews and Samaritans, that neither could have adopted the Pentateuch from the other. It was consequently held that the Samaritan Pentateuch must be traced to copies existing in the kingdom of the ten tribes, which further evidence that the Pentateuch must have existed at the time of the revolt of Jeroboam, and have been of such undisputed divine authority then that even in their schism from Judah and their apostasy from the true worship of God they did not venture to discard it. Additional investigation, however, has shown that this argument is unsound. The Samaritans are not descendants of the ten tribes but of the heathen colonists introduced into the territory of Samaria by the Assyrian monarchs, after the ten tribes had been carried into captivity (2 Kin. xvii. 24). And the Samaritan Pentateuch does not date back of the Babylonish exile. The mutual hatred of the Jews and the Samaritans originated then. The Samaritans, in spite of their foreign birth, claimed to be the brethren of the Jews and proposed to unite with them in rebuilding the temple at Jerusalem (Ezr. iv. 2, 3); but the Jews repudiated their claim and refused their offered assistance. The Samaritans thus repulsed sought in every way to hinder and annoy the Jews and frustrate their enterprise, and finally built a rival temple of their own on the summit of Mount

Gerizim.   Meanwhile, to substantiate their claim of being sprung from ancient Israel, they eagerly accepted the Pentateuch, which was brought them by a renegade priest.

While, therefore, in our present argument no significance can be attached to the Samaritan Pentateuch, we have convincing proof from other sources that the books of Moses were not unknown in the kingdom of the ten tribes. The narrative of the schism in 1 Kin. xii. describes in detail the measures taken by Jeroboam in evident and avowed antagonism to the regulations of the Pentateuch previously established.   And the books of the prophets Hosea and Amos, who exercised their ministry in the ten tribes, in their rebukes and denunciations, in their descriptions of the existing state of things and its contrast with former times, draw upon the facts of the Pentateuch, refer to its laws, and make use of its phrases and forms of speech.   (See note 2, p. 56.)

7. A further argument is furnished by the elementary character of the teachings of the Pentateuch as compared with later Scriptures in which the same truths are more fully expanded.   The development of doctrine in respect to the future state, providential retribution, the spiritual character of true worship, angels, and the Messiah, shows very plainly that the Pentateuch belongs to an earlier period than the book of Job, the Psalms, and the Prophets.

8. The Egyptian words and allusions to Egyptian customs, particularly in the life of Joseph, the narrative of the residence of Israel in Egypt and their journeyings through the wilderness, and in the enactments, institutions, and symbols of the Pentateuch indicate great familiarity on the part of the author and his readers with Egyptian objects, and agree admirably with the Mosaic period; Moses himself having been trained at the court of

Pharaoh and the long servitude of the people having brought them into enforced contact with the various forms of Egyptian life and taught them skill in those arts which were carried in Egypt to great perfection.

These, briefly stated, are the principal arguments of a positive nature for Moses's authorship of the books which bear his name. They are ascribed to him by unanimous and unbroken tradition from the days of Moses himself through the entire period of the Old Testament, and from that onward. This has the inspired and authoritative sanction of the writers of the New Testament and of our Lord himself. It corresponds with the claim which these books make for themselves, corroborated as this is by their adaptation in style and character to their alleged origin, and by the evidence afforded in all the subsequent Scriptures of their existence and recognized authority from the time of their first promulgation, and that even in the schismatical kingdom of Jeroboam in spite of all attempts to throw off its control. And it derives additional confirmation from the progress of doctrine in the Old Testament, which indicates that the Pentateuch belongs to the earliest stage of divine revelation, as well as from the intimate acquaintance with Egyptian objects which it betrays and which is best explained by referring it to the Mosaic age.

The assaults which have been made in modern times upon the Mosaic authorship of the Pentateuch have been mainly in one or other of four distinct lines or in all combined. It is alleged that the Pentateuch cannot be the work of Moses, because (1) It contains anachronisms, inconsistencies, and incongruities. (2) It is of composite origin, and cannot be the work of any one writer. (3) Its three codes belong to different periods and represent different stages of national development. (4) The disregard of its laws shows that they had no existence for ages after the time of Moses. The first of these is the ground of the earliest objections; the second is the position taken by most of the literary critics; the third and fourth represent that of those who follow the lead of Graf and Wellhausen.

THE EARLIEST OBJECTIONS.

Certain ancient heretics denied that Moses wrote the Pentateuch, because they took offence at some of its contents;[1] apart from this his authorship was unchallenged until recent times. The language of Jerome[2] has sometimes been thought to indicate that it was to him a matter of indifference whether the Pentateuch was written by Moses or by Ezra. But his words have no such meaning. He is alluding to the tradition current among the fathers, that the law of Moses perished in the destruction of Jerusalem by Nebuchadnezzar, but was miraculously restored word for word by Ezra, who was divinely inspired for the purpose. Its Mosaic authorship was unquestioned; but whether the story of its miraculous restoration was to be credited or not was to Jerome of no account.

Isaac ben Jasos in the eleventh century is said to have held that Gen. xxxvi. was much later than the time of Moses.[3] Aben Ezra, in the twelfth century, found what he pronounces an insoluble mystery in the words "beyond Jordan" (Deut. i. 1), "Moses wrote" (Deut. xxxi. 9), "The Canaanite was then in the land" (Gen. xii. 6), "In the Mount of Jehovah he shall be seen" (Gen. xxii. 14), and the statement respecting the iron

[1] Clementine Homilies, iii. 46, 47.
[2] Contra Helvidium : Sive Mosen dicere volueris auctorem Pentateuchi, sive Esram instauratorem operis, non recuso.
[3] Studien und Kritiken for 1832, pp. 639 sqq.

bedstead of Og in Deut. iii. 11, from which it has been
inferred, though he does not express himself clearly on
the subject, that he regarded these passages as post-Mosaic interpolations. Peyrerius[1] finds additional ground
of suspicion in the reference to the book of the wars of
the LORD (Num. xxi. 14), to the LORD having given to
Israel the land of their possession (Deut. ii. 12), and
"until this day" (Deut. iii. 14). He also complains of
obscurities, lack of orderly arrangement, repetitions,
omissions, transpositions, and improbable statements.
Spinoza[2] adds as non-Mosaic "Dan" (Gen. xiv. 14, see
Judg. xviii. 29), "the kings that reigned in Edom before
there reigned any king in Israel" (Gen. xxxvi. 31), the
continuance of the manna (Ex. xvi. 35), and Num. xii. 3,
as too laudatory to be from the pen of Moses; and he
remarks that Moses is always spoken of in the third person. His opinion was that Moses wrote his laws from
time to time, which were subsequently collected and the
history inserted by another, the whole being finally
remodelled by Ezra, and called the Books of Moses because he was the principal subject. Hobbes[3] points to
some of the above-mentioned passages as involving anachronisms, and concludes that Moses wrote no part of
the Pentateuch except the laws in Deut. xi.–xxvii. Rich-
ard Simon[4] held that Moses wrote the laws, but the historical portions of the Pentateuch were the work of
scribes or prophets, who were charged with the function
of recording important events. The narratives and genealogies of Genesis were taken by Moses from older writings or oral tradition, though it is impossible to distinguish between what is really from Moses and what is

[1] Systema Theologicum ex Præadamitarum Hypothesi, 1655.
[2] Tractatus Theologico-Politicus, 1670.
[3] In his Leviathan, 1651.
[4] Histoire Critique du Vieux Testament, 1685.

derived from later sources. Le Clerc [1] maintained that the
Pentateuch was written by the priest of Samaria sent by
the king of Assyria to instruct the heathen colonists in
the land of Israel (2 Kings xvii. 26) ; a baseless conjecture, which he subsequently abandoned. He increased
the list of passages assumed to point to another author
than Moses, claiming that the description of the garden
of Eden (Gen. ii. 11, 12) and of the rise of Babylon and
Nineveh (Gen. x. 8) must have been by a writer in Chal-
dea; that " Ur of the Chaldees " (Gen. xi. 28, 31), "the
tower of Eder " (Gen. xxxv. 21, see Mic. iv. 8), " He-
bron " (Gen. xiii. 18, see Josh. xiv. 15), " land of the
Hebrews " (Gen. xl. 15), the word נָבִיא " prophet " (Gen.
xx. 7, see 1 Sam. ix. 9) are all terms of post-Mosaic origin ; and that the explanation respecting Moses and
Aaron (Ex. vi. 25, 26) and respecting the capacity of the
"omer" (xvi. 36) would be superfluous for contemporaries.
He thus deals with the argument from the New Testament : [2] " It will be said, perhaps, that Jesus Christ and
the apostles often quote the Pentateuch under the name
of Moses, and that their authority should be of greater
weight than all our conjectures. But Jesus Christ and
the apostles not having come into the world to teach the
Jews criticism, we must not be surprised if they speak in
accordance with the common opinion. It was of little
consequence to them whether it was Moses or another,
provided the history was true ; and as the common opinion was not prejudicial to piety they took no great pains
to disabuse the Jews."

All these superficial objections were most ably answered by Witsius [3] and Carpzov. [4]

[1] Sentimens de quelques Theologiens de Hollande, 1685. [2] Ibid., p. 126.
[3] Miscellanea Sacra, 2d edition, 1736, I., ch. xiv., An Moses auctor
Pentateuchi.
[4] Introductio ad Libros Canonicos Veteris Testamenti, Editio Nova,
1731, I., pp. 57 sqq.

4

"Beyond Jordan" (Deut. i. 1), said of Moses's position east of the river, does not imply that the writer was in the land of Canaan, as is plain from the ambiguity of the expression. In Num. xxxii. 19 it is in the very same sentence used first of the west and then of the east side of the Jordan; elsewhere it is defined as "beyond Jordan eastward" (Deut. iv. 47, 49; Josh. i. 15; xii. 1; xiii. 8, 27, 32), and "beyond Jordan westward" (Deut. xi. 30; Josh. v. 1; xii. 7; xxii. 7); and in the addresses of Moses it is used alike of the east (Deut. iii. 8) and of the west (vs. 20, 25). This ambiguity is readily explained from the circumstances of the time. Canaan was "beyond Jordan" to Israel encamped in the plains of Moab; and the territory east of the river was "beyond Jordan" to Canaan, the land promised to their fathers, and which they regarded as their proper home.

"The Canaanite was then in the land" (Gen. xii. 6) states that they were in the country in the days of Abraham, but without any implication that they were not there still. "In the Mount of Jehovah he shall be seen" (Gen. xxii. 14) contains no allusion to his manifestation in the temple, which was afterward erected on that very mountain, but is based on his appearance to Abraham in the crisis of his great trial. The bedstead of Og (Deut. iii. 11) is not spoken of as a relic from a former age, but as a memorial of a recent victory. "The book of the wars of Jehovah" (Num. xxi. 14) was no doubt a contemporaneous production celebrating the triumphs gained under almighty leadership, to which Moses here refers. As the territory east of the Jordan had already been conquered and occupied, Moses might well speak (Deut. ii. 12) of the land of Israel's possession, which Jehovah gave to them. The words "unto this day" (Deut. iii. 14) have by many been supposed to be a supplementary gloss subsequently added to the text; but this assump-

tion is scarcely necessary, when it is remembered that
several months had elapsed since the time referred to, and
Havvoth-jair proved to be not only a name imposed by a
successful warrior in the moment of his victory, but one
which had come into general use and promised to be permanent. There is no proof that the " Dan " of Gen. xiv.
14 is the same as that of Judg. xviii. 29 ; or if it be,
there is no difficulty in supposing that in the course of
repeated transcription the name in common use in later
times was substituted for one less familiar which originally stood in the text. The kings of Edom who are
enumerated in Gen. xxxvi. were pre-Mosaic ; and Moses
remarks upon the singular fact that Jacob, who had the
promise of kings among his descendants (Gen. xxxv. 11),
had as yet none, and they were just beginning their national existence, while Esau, to whom no such promise had
been given, already reckoned several. There is nothing in
Ex. xvi. 35 which Moses could not have written ; nor
even in Num. xii. 3, when the circumstances are duly
considered (cf. 1 Cor. xv. 10 ; 2 Cor. xi. 5 ; xii. 11). And
the additional passages urged by Le Clerc have not even
the merit of plausibility. His notion that our Lord and
his apostles accommodated their teaching to the errors
of their time, refutes itself to those who acknowledge
their divine authority. Witsius well says that if they
were not teachers of criticism they were teachers of the
truth.

It should further be observed, that even if it could be
demonstrated that a certain paragraph or paragraphs were
post-Mosaic, this would merely prove that such paragraph or paragraphs could not have belonged to the
Pentateuch as it came from the pen of Moses, not that
the work as a whole did not proceed from him. It is far
easier to assume that some slight additions may here and
there have been made to the text, than to set aside the

multiplied and invincible proofs that the Pentateuch was
the production of Moses.

Note to page 43.

1. The book of Judges records a series of relapses on the part of the
people from the true worship of God, ii.10–12, and the judgments inflicted upon them in consequence by suffering them to fall under the power
of their enemies, ii. 14, 15, as had been foretold Lev. xxvi. 16b, 17.
This extraordinary condition of things led to many seeming departures
from the Mosaic requirements, which have been alleged to show that
the law was not then in existence. That no such conclusion is war-
ranted by the facts of the case will be shown hereafter, see pp. 150 sqq.
For other points of contact with the Pentateuch, comp. i. 1, 2, xx.
.18, and Gen. xlix. 8, Num. ii. 3, x. 14; i. 5, Gen. xiii. 7; i. 17, Deut.
vii. 2 ; i. 20, Num. xiv. 24, Deut. i. 36; ii. 1, Gen. l. 24, xvii. 7 ; ii. 2,
Ex. xxxiv. 12, 13, Deut. vii. 2, 5, Ex. xxiii. 21; ii. 3, Num. xxxiii. 55,
Ex. xxiii. 33, Deut. vii. 16 ; ii. 17, Ex. xxxiv. 15, xxxii. 8; iii. 6, Ex.
xxxiv. 16, Deut. vii. 3, 4 ; v. 4, 5, Deut. xxxiii. 2 ; v. 8, Deut. xxxii.
17; vi. 8, Ex. xx. 2 ; vi. 9, Ex. xiv. 30; vi. 13, Deut. xi. 3–5; vi. 16,
Ex. iii. 12 ; vi. 22, 23, xiii. 22, Ex. xxxiii. 20; vi. 39, Gen. xviii. 32 ;
vii. 18, Num. x. 9 ; viii. 23, Deut xxxiii. 5, the government established
by Moses was a theocracy, the highest civil ruler being a judge, Deut.
xvii. 9, 12 ; viii. 27, superstitious use of the ephod comp. Ex. xxviii. 4,
30 ; xi. 13, Num. xxi. 24–26 ; xi. 15, Deut. ii. 9, 19 ; xi. 16, Num. xiv.
25, xx. 1 ; xi. 17–22, Num. xx. 14, 18, 21, xxi. 21–24 ; xi. 25, Num. xxii.
2 ; xi. 35b, Num. xxx. 2, Deut. xxiii. 24 (E. V. ver. 23) ; xiii. 7, 14,
xvi. 17, Num. vi. 1–5, Deut. xiv. 2 ; xiv. 3, xv. 18, Gen. xvii. 11 ;
xvii. 7–9, xix. 1, Num. xviii. 24, Deut. x. 9 ; xviii. 31, Ex. xl. 2, Josh.
xviii. 1 ; xx. 1, xxi. 10, 13, 16, עֵדָה a word claimed as peculiar to the
Priest Code ; xx. 3, 6, 10, Gen. xxxiv. 7, Lev. xviii. 17, Deut. xxii. 21 ;
xx. 13, Deut. xvii. 12 ; xx. 18, 27, Num. xxvii. 21 ; xx. 26, xxi. 4, Ex.
xx. 24 ; xx. 27, Ex. xxv. 21, 22 ; xx. 28, Num. xxv. 11–13, Deut. x. 8 ;
xx. 48, עִיר מְתֹם as Deut. ii. 34, iii. 6.

Comp. Ruth iii. 12, iv. 3, 4, and Lev. xxv. 25 ; iv. 5, 10, Deut. xxv. 5,
6 ; iv. 11, 12, Gen. xxix., xxx., xxxviii. The obligation of the levirate
marriage has in the course of time been extended from the brother of
the deceased to the nearest relative ; as in the case of Samson and Samuel the Nazarite vow is for life instead of a limited term.

1 Samuel. Comp. i. 11 and Num. vi. 5 ; ii. 2, Ex. xv. 11, Deut.
xxxii. 4, 31 ; ii. 6, Deut. xxxii. 39 ; ii. 13, Deut. xviii. 3 ; ii. 22, Ex.
xxxviii. 8 ; ii. 27, Ex. iv. 27–v. 1, etc.; ii. 28, Ex. xxviii. 1, 4, xxx. 7,
8, Num. xviii. 9, 11 ; ii. 29, iii. 14, sacrifice and meal-offering, x. 8,
etc., burnt-offerings and peace-offerings, vi. 3, trespass-offerings, vii. 9,

whole burnt-offering as Deut. xxxiii. 10 (2 Sam. i. 21, heave-offerings),
implying a fully developed ritual ; iii. 3, iv. 4 (2 Sam. vi. 2), Ex. xxv.
10, 18, 37, Lev. xxiv. 3 ; iv. 3 (2 Sam. xi. 11), Num. x. 35 ; vi. 15, 19,
(2 Sam. vi. 13, xv. 24), Num. iv. 15; viii. 3, Deut. xvi. 19; viii. 5.
Deut. xvii. 14 ; x. 24, Deut. xvii. 15 ; xii. 14, Deut. i. 43, ix. 23 ; xii.
6, 8, Ex. iii. 10, vi. 13; xii. 3, Num. xvi. 15 ; xiii. 9–13, Num. xviii.
4; xv. 2, Ex. xvii. 8, 14, Deut. xxv. 17–19 ; xv. 6, Num. x. 29, 30,
see Judg. i. 16, iv. 11 ; xv. 29, Num. xxiii. 19; xiv. 33, 34, Gen. ix.
4, Lev. iii. 17 ; xxi. 9, xxiii. 6, 9, xxx. 7, Lev. viii. 7, 8; xxviii. 3,
Ex. xxii. 17 (E. V. ver. 18), Deut. xviii. 10, 11 ; xxviii. 6, Num. xii.
6, xxvii. 21.

2 Samuel. Comp. vi. 6, 7, and Num. iv. 15 ; vii. 6, Ex. xl. 19, 24;
vii. 22, Deut. iii. 24 ; vii. 23, Deut. iv. 7, ix. 26, x. 21, xxxiii. 29 ; vii.
24, Ex. vi. 7 ; viii. ; 4, Deut. xvii. 16 ; xi. 4, Lev. xv. 19; xii. 6, Ex.
xxi. 37 (E. V. xxii. 1) ; xii. 9, Num. xv. 31 ; xv. 7–9, Num. xxx. 2;
xxii. 23, Deut. vi. 1.

The books of Kings, it is universally conceded, exhibit an acquaintance with Deuteronomy and with those portions of the Pentateuch
which the critics attribute to JE. It will only be necessary here, therefore, to point out its allusions to the Priest Code. The plan of Solomon's
temple, 1 Kin. vi., vii., is evidently based upon that of the Mosaic
tabernacle, Ex. xxvi., xxvii., xxx.; the golden altar, vii. 48, the brazen
altar, viii. 64, the horns of the altar, i. 50, ii. 28, the lavers, vii. 43, 44,
the table of shew-bread and the candlesticks, with their lamps, vii. 48, 49,
the cherubim upon the walls and in the holiest apartment, vi. 27–29, the
dimensions of the building, and of each apartment, vi. 2, 16, 17, its being
overlaid with gold, vi. 22, and all its vessels made of gold, vii. 48–50, and
the Mosaic ark, the tent of meeting, and all the vessels of the tabernacle
were brought by the priests and Levites and deposited in the temple,
viii. 4. The feast was held in the seventh month, viii. 2, on the fifteenth
day, xii. 32, 33, for seven days and seven days (twice the usual time on
account of the special character of the occasion), viii. 65, and the people
were dismissed on the eighth day, ver. 66, comp. Lev. xxiii. 34, 36. They
had assembled from the entering in of Hamath unto the river of Egypt,
viii. 65, Num. xxxiv. 5, 8. The glory of the Lord filled the temple,
viii. 10, 11, as the tabernacle, Ex. xl. 34, 35; patrimony inalienable,
xxi. 3, Lev. xxv. 23 ; blasphemer to be stoned, xxi. 13, Lev. xxiv. 16 ;
evening meal-offering xviii. 29, morning meal-offering, 2 Kin. iii. 20,
Ex. xxix. 39–41; new moon hallowed, 2 Kin. iv. 23, Num. x. 10,
xxviii. 11 ; laws concerning leprosy, 2 Kin. vii. 3, xv. 5, Lev. xiii. 46 ;
high-priest, xii. 10, xxii. 4, xxiii. 4, Lev. xxi. 10, Num. xxxv. 25 ; trespass-offering and sin-offering, xii. 16, Lev. iv., v. 15 (Deut. xiv. 24, 25) ;
the money of every one that passeth the numbering . . . by his

estimation, xii. 5 (ver 4, see marg. R. V.), Ex. xxx. 13, Lev. xxvii. 2;
meal-offering, drink-offering, brazen altar before the Lord, xvi. 13–15;
unleavened bread the food of priests, xxiii. 9, Lev. vi. 16–18.

The books of the prophets also contain repeated allusions to the Pentateuch, its history, and its institutions.

Joel shows the deepest interest in the ritual service, i. 9, 13, 16, ii.
14–17 ; and recognizes but one sanctuary, ii. 1, 15, iii. 17 (Heb. iv. 17);
comp. i. 10 and Deut. xxviii. 51 ; ii. 2b, Ex. x. 14b ; ii. 3, Gen. ii. 8;
ii. 13, Ex. xxxiv. 6, xxxii. 14 ; ii. 23, 24, Deut. xi. 14.

Isaiah uses the term " law " to denote, or at least as including, God's
authoritative revelation through the prophets, i. 10, ii. 3, v. 24, but also
as additional to the word of God by the prophets, xxx. 9, 10, and of
high antiquity, xxiv. 5, and the test of all professed revelations, viii.
16, 20, since there are prophets that mislead, ix. 15, xxviii. 7, xxix. 10.
To a people strenuous in observing the letter of the Mosaic law, but dis-
regarding its spirit, he announces the law of God to be that the union
of iniquity with the most sacred rites of his worship was intolerable to
the Most High, i. 10–14.   There is in this no depreciation of sacrifice,
for like language is used of prayer, ver. 15, and of worship generally,
xxix. 13 ; and acceptable worship is described under ritual forms, xix.
21, lxvi. 20–23, in contrast with vs. 1–3.   The terms of the ceremonial
law abound in i. 11–13 : sacrifices, burnt-offerings, oblations (meal-offerings), incense ;   fat, blood ; rams, bullocks, lambs, he-goats ;   appear
before me ; court ; new moon, Sabbath, calling of assemblies (convoca-
tions), solemn meeting (assembly), appointed feasts ; abomination.
The vision of ch. vi. gives the most explicit divine sanction to the temple, its altar and its atoning virtue.   Other allusions to the law of sacrifice, implying that it is acceptable and obligatory, xxxiv. 6, xl. 16, xliii.
23, 24, lvi. 7, lx. 7 ; Messiah the true trespass-offering, liii. 10.

Isaiah enforces the law of the unity of the sanctuary, Deut. xii. 5, 6,
by teaching (1) That Zion is Jehovah's dwelling-place, ii. 2, 3, iv. 5,
viii. 18, x. 32, xi. 9, xii. 6, xiv. 32, xxiv. 23, xxviii. 16, xxix. 8, xxxi.
4, 9, lx. 14.   (2) The proper place for Israel's worship, xxvii. 13, xxix.
1, xxx. 29, xxxiii. 20, lxiv. 11, lxvi. 20; no other place of acceptable
worship is ever mentioned or alluded to.   (3) Worship elsewhere, as in
gardens, on lofty places, and under trees, is offensive, i. 29, 30, lvii. 5–7,
lxv. 3, 4, 11.   (4) Altars of man's devising are denounced, xvii. 7, 8,
xxvii. 9.   (5) All such were abolished in Hezekiah's reform, xxxvi. 7.
(6) No objection can be drawn from the altar and the pillar in the land
of Egypt, xix. 19 ; for the pillar was not beside the altar, nor intended
as an idolatrous symbol, so that it was no violation of Lev. xxvi. 1,
Deut. xvi. 21, 22; and an altar in Egypt as a symbol of its worship
paid to Jehovah is more than counterbalanced by pilgrimages to Zion

predicted from other lands, ii. 3, xviii. 7, lvi. 7, lxvi. 20, 23. So that
it is not even certain, whether in the conception of the prophet the restriction of the law in this particular was one day to be relaxed ; much
less is there reason to imagine that this restriction was unknown to
him.

In addition to these recognitions of the laws of the Pentateuch Isaiah
makes allusions to its language and to facts recorded in it.   Thus comp.
i. 2, and Deut. xxxii. 1 ; i. 7, Lev. xxvi. 33 ; i. 9, 10, iii. 9, Sodom and
Gomorrah, Gen. xix. 24, 25, Deut. xxix. 23 (overthrow as i. 7) ; i. 17,
23, Ex. xxii. 21 (E. V. ver. 22), Deut. x. 18, xxvii. 19 ; xi. 15, 16, lxiii.
11–13, passage of the Red Sea and the exodus from Egypt ; xii. 2, Ex.
xv. 2 ; xxiv. 18, Gen. vii. 11 ; xxix. 22, xli. 8, li. 2, lxiii. 16, Abraham
and Sarah ; xxx. 17, Lev. xxvi. 8, Deut. xxxii. 30.

Micah.   Comp. i. 3b, and Deut. xxxiii. 29b ; ii. 1b, Gen. xxxi. 29,
Deut. xxviii. 32b ; ii. 9, Ex. xxii. 21 (E. V. ver. 22) ; ii. 12, iv. 6, 7,
vii. 19, Deut. xxx. 3–5 ; ii. 13b, Ex. xiii. 21 ; iii. 4, Deut. xxxi. 18,
xxxii. 20 ; iv. 4, Lev. xxvi. 6 ; v. 5 (E. V. ver. 6), land of Nimrod,
Gen. x. 8–12 ; vi. 1, 2, Deut. xxxii. 1 ; vi. 4a, Ex. xx. 2, Deut. vii. 8 ;
vi. 4b, Moses, Aaron, and Miriam ; vi. 5, Num. xxii,–xxv. 3, xxxi. 16 ;
v. 6 (E. V. ver. 7), Deut. xxxii. 2 ; vi. 6, 7, exaggeration of legal sacrifices ; vi. 8, Deut. x. 12 ; vi. 10, 11, Deut. xxv. 13–15, Lev. xix. 35,
36 ; vi. 13, Lev. xxvi. 16 ; vi. 14, Lev. xxvi. 26 ; vi. 15, Deut. xxviii.
38–40 ; vii. 14, Num. xxiii. 9, Deut. xxxiii. 28 ; vii. 15, miracles of the
exodus ; vii. 16, Ex. xv. 14–16 ; vii. 17a, Gen. iii. 14 ; vii. 17b, Deut.
xxxii. 24b ; vii. 18a, Ex. xv. 11 ; vii. 18b, Ex. xxxiv. 6, 7.

Jeremiah's familiarity with Deuteronomy is universally conceded ;
it will accordingly be sufficient to show that his book of prophecy is
likewise related to other portions of the Pentateuch.   Comp. ii. 3, and
Lev. xxii. 10, 15, 16 ; ii. 20, Lev. xxvi. 13 ; ii. 34 (see Rev. Ver.), Ex.
xxii. 1 (E. V. ver. 2) ; iv. 23, Gen. i. 2 ; iv. 27, Lev. xxvi. 33 ; v. 2,
Lev. xix. 12 ; vi. 28, ix. 4, Lev. xix. 16 ; vii. 26, Ex. xxxii. 9, xxxiii.
3, 5, xxxiv. 9 ; ix. 4, Gen. xxvii. 36 ; ix. 16, Lev. xxvi. 33 (Deut. xxviii.
36) ; ix. 26 (see Rev. Ver.) Lev. xix. 27, xxi. 5 ; ix. 26b, Lev. xxvi.
41 ; xi. 4, Ex. xix. 5, Lev. xxvi. 12, 13 ; xi. 5, Ex. iii. 8, Num. xiv.
23 ; xiv. 13, Lev. xxvi. 6 ; xiv. 19, 21, Lev. xxvi. 11, 44 ; xv. 1, Ex.
xxxii. 11 ; xvi. 5, Num. vi. 26 ; xvii. 1, Ex. xxxii. 16 ; xvii. 22, Ex.
xx. 8–11 ; xxi. 5, Ex. vi. 1, 6 ; xxviii. 2, 4, Lev. xxvi. 13 ; xxx. 21,
Num. xvi. 5, 9 ; xxxi. 9, Ex. iv. 22 ; xxxi. 15, Gen. xxxv. 19, xxxvii.
35, xlii. 36 ; xxxi. 28, Ex. xxx. 5 ; xxxi. 35, 36, Gen. i. 16, viii. 22 ;
xxxii. 7, 8, Lev. xxv. 25, 49 ; xxxii. 17, 27b, Gen. xviii. 14 ; xxxii.
18, Ex. xx. 5, 6, xxxiv. 6, 7 ; xxxii. 27, Num. xvi. 22, xxvii. 16 ; xxxiii.
22, Gen. xiii. 16, xv. 5, xxii. 17 ; xxxiii. 26, Abraham, Isaac, and Jacob ; xxxiv. 13, Ex. xx. 2, xxiv. 7 ; xxxiv. 18, 19, Gen. xv. 17 ; xxxvi.

14, Ex. xxi. 2 ; xlviii. 45, 46, Num. xxi. 28, 29; xlix. 16, Num. xxiv. 21 ; xlix. 18, l. 40, Gen. xix. 25.

Psalm xc., which is in its title ascribed to Moses, abounds in allusions to the statements of the Pentateuch and in coincidences of language; see the Commentary of Delitzsch. The following may be noted in those Psalms of the first three books, which are in their titles ascribed to David (the number of each verse in the English version is commonly one less than in the Hebrew). Comp. iii. 4, and Gen. xv. 1 ; iv. 6, li. 21, Deut. xxxiii. 19 ; iv. 7, Num. vi. 25, 26 ; iv. 9, Lev. xxv. 18, 19, Deut. xxxiii. 28 ; vii. 13, 14, Deut. xxxii. 23, 41, 42 ; viii. 7-9, Gen. i. 26 ; ix. 6, Deut. ix. 14 ; ix. 13, Gen. ix. 5 ; ix. 17, Ex. vii. 4b, 5 ; xi. 6, Gen. xix. 24 ; xiii. 2, Deut. xxxi. 18 ; xiv. 1, Gen. vi. 11, 12 ; xv. 5, Ex. xxii. 25, xxiii. 8 ; xvi. 4, Ex. xxiii. 13 ; xvi. 5, Num. xviii. 20, Deut. x. 9; xvii. 8, Deut. xxxii. 10; xviii. 16, Ex. xv. 8; xviii. 27b, Lev. xxvi. 23b, 24a ; xviii. 31a, 32, Deut. xxxii. 4a, 37, 39 ; xviii. 34b, Deut. xxxii. 13a, xxxiii. 29b ; xviii. 45b, Deut. xxxiii. 29b ; xix. contrasts the glory of God as seen in the heavens with that of the law, testimony, statutes, commandments, and judgments of Jehovah, Lev. xxvi. 46, xxvii. 34, Ex. xxv. 16; xx. 6, Ex. xvii. 15, Jehovah my banner ; xxiv. 1, Ex. ix. 29b, xix. 5b ; xxiv. 2, Gen. i. 9 ; xxv. 4, Ex. xxxiii. 13 ; xxvi. 6, Ex. xxx. 19-21; xxvii. 1, Ex. xv. 2 ; xxviii. 9, Deut. ix. 29 ; xxix. 6, Sirion, Deut. iii. 9; xxix. 10, flood, Gen. vi. 17 ; xxxi. 9a, Deut. xxxii. 30 ; xxxi. 16, Num. vi. 25 ; xxxiv. 17, Lev. xvii. 10 ; xxxv. 10, Ex. xv. 11 ; xxxvii. 26, Deut. xxviii. 12 ; xxxvii. 31, Deut. vi. 6 ; xxxix. 13b, Lev. xxv. 23b; xl. 7, Ex. xxi. 6?; xl. 8, the volume of the book is the law, which in requiring sacrifice intends much more than the outward form of sacrifice, ver. 7; it lays its real demand upon the person of the offerer himself : li. 9, hyssop, Lev. xiv. 4, Num. xix. 6, 18 ; lv. 16, Num. xvi. 30 ; lx. 9, Gen. xlix. 10 ; lx. 14, Num. xxiv. 18 ; lxiii. 12, Deut. vi. 13 ; lxviii. 2, Num. x. 35 ; lxviii. 8, 9, 18, Sinai ; lxix. 29, Ex. xxxii. 32 ; lxxxvi. 8, 10, Ex. xv. 11, Deut. xxxii. 39 ; lxxxvi. 15, Ex. xxxiv. 6.

On the traces of the Pentateuch in later books see Hävernick, Einleitung in das Alte Testament (Introduction to the Old Testament), I. §§ 136–142. Keil, Einleitung in A. T. § 34. Caspari, Beiträge zur Einleitung in Jesaia (Contributions to the Introduction to Isaiah), pp. 204 sqq. Caspari, "Ueber Micha," pp. 419 sqq. Kueper, Jeremias Librorum Sacrorum Interpres atque Vindex, pp. 1–51.

Note to page 45.

2. Allusions in Hosea and Amos to the facts recorded in the Pentateuch: Comp. Hos. i. 10, and Gen. xxii. 17, xxxii. 12 ; xi. 8, Deut. xxix. 23 ; xii. 3a, Gen. xxv. 26 ; xii. 3b, 4a, Gen. xxxii. 28 ; xii. 4b,

Gen. xxviii. 12-19, xxxv. 6-13; xii. 12, Jacob fled to Padan-aram,
served for a wife, and kept sheep ; ii. 15b, xi. 1, xiii. 5, exodus from
Egypt and life in the wilderness ; ix. 10, Num. xxv. 3 ; the places of
idolatrous worship were such as were made sacred by events in the history of their fathers, iv. 15, Josh. iv. 20, Gen. xxviii. 19 (Bethel the
house of God is converted into Beth-aven, house of wickedness); xii.
11, Gen. xxxi. 48 ; Amos, v. 8, Gen. vii. 11 ; iv. 11, Gen. xix. 24, 25 ;
i. 11, Edom, Israel's brother, Gen. xxv. 27, Deut. xxiii. 7; iv. 4, v. 5,
places of idolatry hallowed by events in the time of their forefathers ;
ii. 10, iii. 1, v. 25, 26, exodus from Egypt, and forty years in the wilderness, and idolatry there, Deut. v. 6, xxix. 5, Lev. xvii. 7 ; iii. 2,
Deut. xiv. 2 ; vi. 14, Num. xxxiv. 5, 8 ; ii. 9, stature of the Amorites,
Num. xiii. 32, 33, Deut. i, 20, 28.

References to its laws : Hosea constantly sets forth the relation between
Jehovah and Israel under the emblem of a marriage, comp. Ex. xx. 5,
xxxiv. 14-16, Lev. xvii. 7, xx. 5, 6. Israel is an unfaithful wife, who
had responded to her lord in former days, when she came up out of
Egypt, ii. 15, Ex. xxiv. 7, but had since abandoned him for other lov-
ers, ch. i.- iii., Baal and the calves, xiii. 1, 2 ; she has broken her covenant, has dealt treacherously, v. 7, vi. 7 ; has backslidden, iv. 16, xi.
7, xiv. 4 ; is repeating the atrocity of Gibeah, ix. 9, x. 9 ; is shamelessly
sacrificing on the hills and under shady trees, iv. 13, Deut. xii. 2 ;
Israel had an extensive written law, Hos. viii. 12 (see a discussion of
this passage in the *Presbyterian Review* for October, 1886), which they
had disobeyed, iv. 6, viii. 1 ; the annual feasts, new-moons, sabbaths,
and festive assemblies were observed in Israel, and held in high esteem,
and occupied a prominent place in the life of the people, so that their
abolition would be reckoned a serious disaster, Hos. ii. 11, ix. 5, xii. 9,
Am. v. 21, viii. 5 ; they had burnt-offerings, meal-offerings, peace-
offerings, Am. v. 22, Hos. viii. 13 ; thank-offerings, free-will-offerings,
Am. iv. 5 ; drink-offerings, Hos. ix. 4 ; the daily morning sacrifice, Am.
iv. 4 ; Hos. iv. 8, alludes to the law of the sin-offering ; Hos. ix. 3, 4,
to the law of clean and unclean meats ; viii. 11, xii. 11, the sin of mul-
tiplying altars implies the law of the unity of the sanctuary, Deut. xii.
5,6 ; v. 10, removing landmarks, Deut. xix. 14, xxvii. 17; iv. 4, the
final reference of causes in dispute to the priest, refusal to hear whom
was a capital offence, Deut. xvii. 12 ; viii. 13, ix. 3, penalty of a return
to Egypt, Deut. xxviii. 68 ; ix. 4, defilement from the dead, Num. xix.
14, 22, Deut. xxvi. 14 ; x. 11, the ox not to be muzzled when treading
out corn, Deut. xxv. 4 ; vi. 9, זִמָּה is a technical word of the Holiness
Laws, Lev. xviii. 17 ; xiv. 3, mercy for the fatherless, Ex. xxii. 21, 22,
(E. V. vs. 22, 23), Deut. x. 18 ; vi. 11, Am. ix. 14, God returns to the
captivity of his people, Deut. xxx. 3 ; Amos, though delivering his

message in Bethel, knows but one sanctuary, that in Zion, i. 2 ; ii. 7, the law of incest, Lev. xx. 11, Deut. xxii. 30 ; ii. 11, 12, Nazarites, Num. vi. 2, 3, and prophets, Deut. xviii. 15 ; iv. 4, triennial tithes, Deut. xiv. 28, xxvi. 12, for which in their excess of zeal they may substitute tithes every three days ; viii. 5, falsifying the ephah, shekel, and balances, Lev. xix. 36, Deut. xxv. 13–15.

Coincidences of thought or expression : Comp. Hos. ii. 17, and Ex. xxiii. 13 ; iii. 1, look to other gods, Deut. xxxi. 18 (Heb.) ; v. 14–vi. 1, Deut. iv. 29, 30, xxxii. 39 ; iv. 10, Lev. xxvi. 26 ; xi. 1, Ex. iv. 22, 23 ; xii. 5, Ex. iii. 15 ; xiii. 6, Deut. viii. 12–14 ; Am. ii. 7, to profane my holy name, Lev. xx. 3 ; iv. 6, 8, Deut. xxviii. 48 ; iv. 9, Deut. xxviii. 22 ; iv. 10, Deut. xxviii. 60 ; iv. 6, 8, 9, 10, Deut. iv. 30 ; v. 11, ix. 14, Deut. xxviii. 30, 39 ; vi. 12, gall and wormwood, Deut. xxix. 18 ; ix. 13, Lev. xxvi. 5.

For traces of the Pentateuch in the kingdom of Israel, whether in Hosea, Amos, or the Books of Kings, see Hengstenberg, " Authentie des Pentateuches," I. pp. 48–180.

IV

THE UNITY OF THE PENTATEUCH

The second objection which has been urged against the Mosaic origin of the Pentateuch, affects its form rather than its contents. It is affirmed that such is the constitution of the Pentateuch as to evince that it is not the continuous composition of any one writer, but that it is compacted of parts of diverse origin, the products of different writers, themselves long posterior to the Mosaic age; and consequently the Pentateuch, though it may contain some Mosaic elements, cannot in its present form have proceeded from Moses, but must belong to a much later period. This objection is primarily directed against the unity of the Pentateuch, and only secondarily against its authenticity.

In order to render intelligible the nature of the partition hypotheses, with which we shall have to deal, the nomenclature which they employ, and their application to the Pentateuch, it will be necessary first to state precisely what is meant by the unity for which we contend, and then give a brief account of the origin and history of those hypotheses by which it has been impugned, and the several forms which they have successively assumed.

By the unity of the Pentateuch is meant that it is in its present form one continuous work, the product of a single writer. This is not opposed to the idea of his having had before him written sources in any number or variety, from which he may have drawn his materials, provided the composition was his own. It is of no consequence, so far as our present inquiry is concerned, whether the facts related were learned from pre-existing writings, or from credible tradition, or from his own personal knowledge, or from immediate divine revelation. From whatever source the materials may have been gathered, if all has been cast into the mould of the writer's own thoughts, presented from his point of view, and arranged upon a plan and method of his own, the work possesses the unity which we maintain. Thus Bancroft's " History of the United States " rests upon a multitude of authorities which its author consulted in the course of its preparation ; the facts which it records were drawn from a great variety of pre-existing written sources ; and yet, as we possess it, it is the product of one writer, who first made himself thoroughly acquainted with his subject, and then elaborated it in his own language and according to his own preconceived plan. It would have been very different, if his care had simply been to weave together his authorities in the form of a continuous narrative, retaining in all cases their exact language, but incorporating one into another or supplementing one by another, and thus allowing each of his sources in turn to speak for itself. In this case it would not have been Bancroft's history. He would have been merely the compiler of a work consisting of a series of extracts from various authors. Such a narrative has been made by harmonists of the Gospel history. They have framed an account of all the recorded facts by piecing together extracts from the several gospels arranged in what is conceived to be their true chronological order. And the result is not a new Gospel history based upon the several Gospels, nor is it the original Gospel either of Matthew, Mark, Luke, or John ; but it is a compound of the whole of them ; and it can be taken apart paragraph by paragraph, or sentence by sentence, and each portion assigned to the particular Gospel from which it was drawn.

Now the question respecting the unity of the Pentateuch is whether it is a continuous production from a single pen, whatever may have been the sources from which the materials were taken, or whether it is a composite production, made up from various writings woven together, the several portions of which are still capable of being distinguished, separated, and assigned to their respective originals.

DOCUMENT HYPOTHESIS.

The not improbable conjecture was expressed at an early period that there were ante-Mosaic records, to which Moses had access, and of which he made use in preparing the book of Genesis. The history of such a remote antiquity would seem to be better accredited if it had a written basis to rest upon than if it had been drawn solely from oral tradition. Thus the eminent orthodox theologian and commentator Vitringa, expressed the opinion in 1707, in the interest of the credibility of Genesis, that Moses collected, digested, embellished, and supplemented the records left by the fathers and preserved among the Israelites. The peculiarity of the critical hypothesis, with which we are now concerned, however, is the contention that Genesis was not merely based upon pre-existing writings, but that it was framed out of those writings, which were incorporated in it and simply pieced together, so that each section and paragraph and sentence preserved still its original style and texture, indicative of the source from which it came; and that by means of these criteria the book of Genesis can be taken apart and its original sources reproduced. The

first suggestion of this possibility and the first attempt
actually to realize it by decomposing the book into the
prior documents supposed to have been embedded in it,
was made in 1753 by Astruc, a French physician of considerable learning, but of profligate life, in a treatise entitled " Conjectures Concerning the Original Memoranda
which it appears Moses used to Compose the Book of
Genesis." [1] This hypothesis was adopted and elaborated
with great learning and ingenuity by Eichhorn,[2] the distinguished professor of Oriental literature at Göttingen,
to whose skilful advocacy it owed much of its sudden
popularity.

[1] Conjectures sur les Mémoires Originaux, dont it paroit que Moyse
s'est servi pour composer le Livre de la Genèse. Avec des Remarques,
qui appuient ou qui éclaircissent ces Conjectures. This was published
anonymously at Brussels. For an account of the life and character of
the author see the Article Jean Astruc, by Dr. Howard Osgood, in
The Presbyterian and Reformed Review, for January, 1892. Astruc
assumes two principal documents, which were used throughout, and are
distinguished by the employment of Elohim and Jehovah respectively ;
also ten minor documents relating chiefly to foreign nations, and not
immediately affecting the Hebrew people, in which no name of God is
found. These may have been of considerable extent, though Moses
only had occasion to make one small extract from each. With these he
classes likewise the story of Dinah, ch. xxxiv., and the extra document
to account for the triple repetitions in vii. 18-20 and 21-23 in the narrative of the flood. The advantages which he claims for his hypothesis are that it will account for the alternation of the divine names as well
as for the repetitions and displacements in the narrative. Occasional
departures from the exact chronological order are in his view attributable, not to any negligence on the part of Moses, but to the mistakes of
transcribers. These documents were, as he supposes, originally arranged in parallel columns after the manner of Origen's Hexapla ; but
the transcribers, who copied them in one continuous text, sometimes
inserted paragraphs in the wrong places.

[2] Einleitung in das Alte Testament, von Johann Gottfried Eichhorn.
First edition, 1782 ; 4th edition, 1823. He steadfastly insists that
Moses is the compiler of Genesis, and the author of the rest of the Pentateuch, some interpolations excepted. Gramberg, whose Libri Gene-
seos secundum fontes rite dignoscendos Adumbratio Nova was published

1. The primary basis of this extraordinary hypothesis was found in the remarkable manner in which the divine names Elohim (the Hebrew term for God) and Jehovah are used, particularly in the earliest portions of Genesis, whole paragraphs and even long sections making almost exclusive use of one of these names, while the alternate sections make a similarly exclusive use of the other. Thus in Gen. i. 1–ii. 3, Elohim occurs in almost every verse, but no other name of God than this. But in ii. 4–iii. 24, God is with few exceptions called Jehovah Elohim, and in ch. iv. Jehovah. Then in ch. v. we find Elohim again ; in vi. 1–8, Jehovah, and in the rest of ch. vi., Elohim, and so on. This singular alternation was remarked upon by some of the early Christian fathers,[1] who offered an explanation founded upon the Greek and Latin equivalents of these names, but which is not applicable to the Hebrew terms themselves. Astruc's assumption was that it was due to the peculiar style of different writers, one of whom was in the habit of using Elohim, and another in the habit of using Jehovah, when speaking of God. All those paragraphs and sections which exclusively or predominantly employ the name Elohim were accordingly attributed to a writer denominated from this circumstance the Elohist ; and when these paragraphs were singled out and put together, they constituted what was called the Elohist document. The other writer was known as the Jehovist, and the sections attributed to him made up the Jehovist document. It

in 1828, substitutes for this faithful compiler an unknown Redactor, who in combining the Elohist and Jehovist makes frequent changes and additions of his own.

[1] Thus Tertullian adv. Hermogenem, ch. 3, remarks that the Most High is simply called " God " until the world was made, and his intelgent creature, man, over whom he had dominion, after which he is likewise called " LORD." See also Augustin, De Genesi ad Literam, viii. 11.

was accordingly held that Genesis consisted of sections taken alternately from two distinct documents by authors of known proclivities, so far at least as their preference for or exclusive use of one or other of the divine names, and which existed and circulated in their separate state until they were combined as they are at present. This hypothesis is hence known as the document hypothesis, since it assumes as the sources of Genesis distinct and continuous documents, which are still traceable in the book from the beginning to the end. And the first argument adduced in its support, as already stated, is the interchange of divine names, each of which is erected into the criterion of a separate document.

2. A second argument was drawn from the alleged fact that when the Elohim sections are sundered out and put together, they form a regularly constructed and continuous narrative without any apparent breaks or chasms, whence it is inferred that they originally constituted one document distinct from the intercalated Jehovah sections. The same thing was affirmed, though with more hesitation and less appearance of plausibility, of the Jehovah sections likewise; when these are singled out and severed from the passages containing the name Elohim, they form a tolerably well-connected document likewise.

3. A third argument was drawn from parallel passages in the two documents. The same event, it is alleged, is in repeated instances found twice narrated in successive sections of Genesis, once in an Elohist section, and again with some modifications or variations in a Jehovist section. This is regarded as proof positive that Genesis is not one continuous narrative, but that it is made up from two different histories. The compiler instead of framing a new narrative which should comprehend all the particulars stated in both accounts, or blending the two accounts by incorporating sentences from one in the

body of the other, has preserved both entire, each in its integrity and in its own proper form, by first giving the account of the matter as it was to be found in one document, and subsequently inserting the account found in the other. Thus Gen. i. 1–ii. 3 contains the account of the creation as given by the Elohist; but although this states how the world was made, and plants and animals and men were formed upon it, the Jehovist section, ii. 4, etc., introduces a fresh account of the making of the man and the woman, the production of trees from the ground, and the formation of the inferior animals. This repetition betrays, it is said, that we here have before us not one account of the creation by a single writer, but two separate accounts by different writers. So in the narrative of the flood; there is first an account by the Jehovist, vi. 1–8, of the wickedness of man and of Jehovah's purpose to destroy the earth; then follows, vi. 9–22, the Elohist's statement of the wickedness of man and God's purpose to destroy the earth, together with God's command to Noah to build the ark and go into it with his family, and take some of all living animals into it; in vii. 1–5, the Jehovist tells that Jehovah commanded Noah to go with his family into the ark, and to take every variety of animals with him.

4. A fourth argument is drawn from the diversity of style, diction, ideas, and aim which characterize these two documents. It is alleged that when these component parts of Genesis are separated and examined apart, each will be found to be characterized by all the marks which indicate diversity of origin and authorship. It is confidently affirmed that, wherever the Elohim sections occur throughout Genesis, they have certain peculiarities of diction and style which clearly distinguish them from the Jehovah sections; and these again have their own distinctive characteristics. The preference for one di-

vine name above another, which has already been spoken of as a criterion, does not stand alone. There are besides numerous words and phrases that are currently used by the Elohist which the Jehovist never employs, and *vice versa*. Thus the Elohist, in ch. i., uses the phrase "beast of the earth," and speaks of the earth bringing forth plants, while the Jehovist, in ch. ii., says "beasts of the field" and "plant of the field." The Elohist, in ch. i., repeatedly uses the word "create"; he speaks of God creating the heavens and the earth, creating the whales, and creating man. The Jehovist, in ch. ii., speaks instead of Jehovah forming man and forming the beasts. The Elohist (ch. i.) speaks of man as male and female; the Jehovist (ch. ii.) says instead the man and his wife. The style of the two writers is equally marked; that of the Elohist is formal, verbose, and repetitious; that of the Jehovist is easy and flowing. In ch. i. the same stereotyped phrases recur again and again, and particulars are enumerated instead of including all under a general term. Thus ver. 25, " God made the beast of the earth after his kind, and cattle after their kind, and every creeping thing that creepeth upon the earth after his kind." And ver. 27, " God created man in his own image, in the image of God created he him; male and female created he them." The Elohist gives God's command to Noah in detail (vi. 18), "Thou shalt come into the ark; thou, and thy sons, and thy wife, and thy sons' wives with thee;" the Jehovist simply says, (vii. 1), "Come thou and all thy house into the ark."

Along with these peculiarities of diction and style, and corroborating the conclusion drawn from them, is the diversity in the ideas and scope of the two writers. Thus the Jehovist makes frequent mention of altars and sacrifices in the pre-Mosaic period; the Elohist is silent respecting them until their establishment at Sinai. It is the Jehovist who records the primeval sacrifice of Cain and Abel, of which the Elohist says nothing. The Elohist speaks, in v. 22, of Enoch walking with God, and vi. 9, of Noah walking with God, but though he gives (ch. ix.) a detailed account of God's blessing Noah, and his covenant with him after he came out of the ark, he says nothing of Noah's sacrifice, which the Jehovist records (viii. 20, etc). The divine direction to Noah to take animals into the ark is given by the Elohist only in general terms; God bade him take two of every sort (vi. 19, etc.). But the Jehovist informs us more minutely of the distinction of clean and unclean animals which then existed, and that Jehovah bade Noah take two of each species of the latter, but seven of the former, vii. 2.

These arguments, derived from the alternate use of the divine names, from the alleged continuity of each document taken separately, from parallel passages, and from the characteristic differences of the two writers, appeared to lend so much plausibility to the Document Hypothesis that it speedily rose to great celebrity, and was very widely adopted; and many able and distinguished critics became its advocates. As at first propounded it did not conflict with the Mosaic authorship of the Pentateuch. Its earliest defenders, so far from impugning the authorship of Moses, were strenuous in maintaining it. So long as the hypothesis was confined to Genesis, to which it was at first applied, there was no difficulty in assuming that Moses may have incorporated in his history of that early period these pre-existing documents in any way consistent with his truth and inspiration.

It was not long, however, before it was discovered that the hypothesis was capable of being applied likewise to the remaining books of the Pentateuch. This extension of the hypothesis brought it for the first time into collision with the traditional belief of the Mosaic authorship;

and this, with its various modifications, has since been one of the favorite and principal weapons of those who deny that it was written by Moses. If the entire Pentateuch is a compilation from pre-existing documents, it was plausibly inferred that it must be post-Mosaic. For the documents themselves, inasmuch as they contained the record of Moses's own times, could not have been older than the Mosaic age. And if the Pentateuch was subsequent to them, and framed out of them, it seemed natural to refer it to a still later period; though, it should be observed, that this by no means necessarily follows. Even if the composite character of the Pentateuch could be established on purely literary grounds, we might still suppose that the memoranda from which it was prepared were drawn up under Moses's direction and with his approval, and were either put together in their present form by himself, or at least that the completed work passed under his eye and received his sanction; so that it would still be possible to vindicate its Mosaic origin and authority, unless indeed the primary documents themselves belong to a later time than that of Moses, which can never be proved.

The critics who have held this hypothesis, however, commonly do regard them as post-Mosaic; and hence they claim that it affords ocular demonstration that the books traditionally ascribed to Moses are not his. And to corroborate this conclusion they appeal to Exodus vi. 3, where God says to Moses, " I appeared unto Abraham, unto Isaac, and unto Jacob, as God Almighty, but by my name JEHOVAH I was not known to them." They understand this to be a distinct declaration that the name Jehovah was unknown to the patriarchs, being of later date than the time in which they lived, and that it first came into use in the days of Moses. It hence followed as a logical necessity that the Jehovist document, according to the testimony of this passage, was certainly not prior to the time of Moses, for it employs a name which had no existence previously. And it was plausibly urged that this document was probably post-Mosaic, for it is chargeable with the anachronism of putting into the mouths of the patriarchs the name Jehovah, which did not then exist. This was thought to be contradictory to the Elohist statement above cited, and to betray a writer belonging to a period when the name Jehovah had become so familiar and so universal that its recent origin was forgotten, and he unconsciously transfers to patriarchal times a designation current in his own.

This anachronism of the Jehovist led to the suspicion of others; and since, as has already been stated, it is this document which makes mention of patriarchal altars and sacrifices that are never referred to by the Elohist, it was suspected that here again he had improperly transferred to the patriarchal age the usages of his own time, while the Elohist gave a more accurate representation of that early period as it really was. This was esteemed, if not a contradiction, yet a contrariety between the two accounts, a diversity in the mode of conceiving the period whose history they are recording, which reflects the different personality of the two writers, the views which they entertained, and the influences under which they had been trained.

These diversities between the Jehovist and the Elohist took on more and more the character of contradictions, as the credit of the Jehovist for veracity and accuracy was held in less and less esteem. Every superficial difficulty was made the pretext for fresh charges of anachronisms, inaccuracies, and contradictions. The text was tortured to bring forth difficulties where none appeared. An especially fruitful source was found in alleged parallel passages in the two documents. These

were greatly multiplied by pressing into the service nar-
rations of matters quite distinct, but which bore a general
resemblance to each other. The points of resemblance were
paraded in proof that the matters referred to were identical ; and then the diversities in the two accounts were
pointed out as so many contradictions between them,
which betrayed the legendary and unreliable character of
one or both the narratives. Thus because some of the
descendants of Cain, whose genealogy is recorded by the
Jehovist (Gen. iv. 17–22), bear the same or similar names
with descendants of Seth recorded by the Elohist (ch. v.),
Enoch, Irad, Methusaël, and Lamech of one table corresponding to Jared, Enoch, Methuselah, and Lamech of
the other, it was concluded that these are only variants
of the same identical genealogy, which one writer has attached to one of the sons of Adam, and the other to another ; and that every divergence in the two lists is a
discrepancy involving an error on one side or on the
other, if not in both. So in ch. xii. the Jehovist tells how
Abram, apprehensive that the monarch of the country in
which he was would be attracted by his wife's beauty,
prevaricated by saying that she was his sister, what per-
ils thence arose to both, and how they were finally extri-
cated. In ch. xx. the Elohist relates a similar story of
prevarication, peril, and deliverance. The same event, it
is alleged, must be the basis of both accounts, but there
is a hopeless contradiction between them. The former
declares that the occurrence took place in Egypt, and
that Pharaoh was a party to the transaction ; the latter
transfers the scene to the land of the Philistines and the
court of Abimelech. And to complicate the matter still
further, the Jehovist gives yet another version of the
same story in ch. xxvi., according to which it was not
Abram but Isaac who thus declared his wife to be his
sister, running an imminent hazard by so doing, but

making a fortunate escape. According to the Elohist (xxi. 22–32), Abraham had a difficulty with Abimelech in respect to a well of water, which was amicably settled by a covenant, in memory of which he gave name to Beersheba. The Jehovist (xxvi. 17–33) relates a similar story of strife concerning wells, a visit by Abimelech, an agreement with him, and the naming of Beersheba in consequence; but he says that it was not Abraham but Isaac who was concerned in it.

FRAGMENT HYPOTHESIS.

Meanwhile a more extreme disintegration found favor with Vater [1] (1805), Hartmann [2] (1831), and others, who advocated what is known as the Fragment Hypothesis. This may be fitly characterized as the Document Hypothesis run mad. It is a *reductio ad absurdum* furnished by the more consistent and thorough-going application of the principles and methods of its predecessor. Instead of two continuous documents pieced together, paragraph by paragraph, to constitute the Pentateuch as we now have it, each paragraph or section is now traced to a separate and independent source. The compiler was not limited to two writings covering alike the entire

[1] Commentar über den Pentateuch von Johann Severin Vater. 1st and 2d Part, 1802 ; 3d Part, 1805. This embodies many of the Explanatory Notes and Critical Remarks of Rev. Alexander Geddes, with whose views he is in entire accord. Vater finds that Genesis is composed of thirty-eight fragments, varying in length from four or five verses to several chapters. The other books of the Pentateuch are similarly disintegrated. In fact, the legislation is the favorite domain of the Fragment Hypothesis, as the history furnishes the principal material for the Document Hypothesis.

[2] Historisch-kritische Forschungen über die Bildung, das Zeitalter und den Plan der fünf Bücher Mose's, nebst einer beurtheilenden Einleitung und einer genauen Charakteristik der hebräischen Sagen und Mythen, von Anton Theodor Hartmann.

period that he proposed to treat, but had before him all that he could gather of every sort relating to his subject, some of which possibly were mere scraps, others of larger compass, some recording, it may be, but a single incident, others more comprehensive, and he adopted one passage from one, another from another, and so on throughout. Sometimes two or more fragments may have been taken from the same original work, but this cannot be positively affirmed. And it would be vain to attempt to inquire into the extent, character, and aim of the writings from which they were severally extracted. All that we know of them is derived from such portions as the compiler has seen fit to preserve.

The arguments adduced in support of the Fragment Hypothesis were substantially identical with those which had been urged in favor of the Document Hypothesis. And assuming the soundness of those arguments, this is the inevitable consequence. Admit the legitimacy of this disintegrating process, and there is no limit to which it may not be carried at the pleasure of the operator; and it might be added, there is no work to which it might not be applied. Any book in the Bible, or out of the Bible, could be sliced and splintered in the same way and by the same method of argument. Let a similarly minute and searching examination be instituted into the contents of any modern book. Let any one page be compared with any other, and every word, and form of expression, and grammatical construction, and rhetorical figure in one that does not occur in the other be noted as difference of diction and style; let every incident in one that has its counterpart in the other be paraded as a parallel section evidencing diversity of origin and authorship, and every conception in one which has not its counterpart in the other as establishing a diversity in the ideas of the authors of the two pages respectively;

let every conclusion arrived at on one page that does not appear on the other argue different tendencies in the two writers, different aims with which, and different influences under which, they severally wrote, and nothing would be easier, if this method of proof be allowed, than to demonstrate that each successive page came from a different pen.

The very same process by which the Pentateuch is decomposed into documents, can with like facility divide these documents, and subdivide them, and then subdivide them again. Indeed the advocates of the Document Hypothesis may here be summoned as witnesses against themselves. They currently admit different Elohists and Jehovists, and successive variant editions of each document, and a whole school of priestly and Deuteronomic diaskeuasts and redactors, thus rivalling in their refinements the multitudinous array of the fragmentary critics. And in fact the extent to which either may go in this direction is determined by purely subjective considerations. The only limitation is that imposed by the taste or fancy of the critic. If the repetitions or parallel sections, alleged to be found in the Pentateuch, require the assumption of distinct documents, like repetitions occurring in each individual document prove it to be composite. The very same sort of contrarieties or contradictions which are made a pretext for sundering the Pentateuch, can furnish an equally plausible reason for sundering each of the documents. And if certain criteria are regarded as characteristic of a given document, and their absence from sections attributed to the other is held to prove that they are by a different hand from the former, why does not the same rule apply to the numerous sections of the first-named document, from which its own so-called characteristic words and phrases are likewise absent ?

The titles and subscriptions attached to genealogies and legal sections supplied an additional argument, of which the advocates of the Fragment Hypothesis sought to avail themselves. Such titles as the following are prefixed to indicate the subject of the section that follows : " These are the generations of the heavens and of the earth," Gen. ii. 4. " This is the book of the generations of Adam," v. 1. " These are the names of the sons of Levi according to their generations," Ex. vi. 16. " This is the law of the trespass-offering," Lev. vii. 1. " This is the law of the sacrifice of peace-offerings," ver. 11. " These are the journeys of the children of Israel," Num. xxxiii. 1. Or subscriptions are added at the close suggestive of the contents of the section that precedes, such as " These are the families of the sons of Noah after their generations in their nations," Gen. x. 32. " These be the sons of Leah," xlvi. 15. " These are the sons of Zilpah," ver. 18. " These are the sons of Rachel," ver. 22. " This is the law of the burnt-offering, of the meal-offering, and of the sin-offering," etc., Lev. vii. 37, 38. " This is the law of the plague of leprosy," etc., xiii. 59. These indicate divisions in the subject-matter, and mark the beginning or end of paragraphs or sections, and contribute to clearness by brief statements of their general purport, but they do not prove that these sections ever had a separate and independent existence apart from the book in which they are now found, or that different sections proceeded from different authors, any more than a like conclusion could be drawn from the books and chapters into which modern works are divided.

The extravagance and absurdity of the Fragment Hypothesis could not long escape detection, for—

1. It involves the assumption of a numerous body of writings regarding the Mosaic and ante-Mosaic periods

of which there is no other evidence, and which is out of all proportion to the probabilities of the case. Every several paragraph or section is supposed to represent a distinct work, implying a literary activity and a fertility of authorship which is not only assumed on slender and inadequate grounds, but of which not another fragment survives, to which no allusion is made, whether in the Pentateuch itself or elsewhere, and not a hint or a trace is anywhere preserved of its ever having existed.

2. A congeries of fragments borrowed from diverse quarters could only form a body of disconnected anecdotes or a heterogeneous miscellany. It could not possibly result in the production of such a work as the Pentateuch, which is a coherent whole, possessing orderly arrangement in accordance with a well-devised plan, which is consistently carried out, with a continuous and connected narrative, with no abrupt transitions, and no such contrasts or discords as would inevitably arise from piecing together what was independently conceived and written by different persons at different times, and with no regard to mutual adjustment. As in oriental writings generally the successive portions are more loosely bound together in outward form than is customary in modern occidental style; but the matter of the record is throughout continuous, and one constant aim is steadfastly pursued. The breaks and interruptions which are alleged to exist in the narrative, such as the failure to record in full the abode in Egypt, the private life of Moses, or the forty years' wandering in the wilderness, are no indications of a lack of unity, but the reverse; for they show with what tenacity the writer adhered to his proper theme, and excluded everything which did not belong to it.

3. Still further, the Pentateuch is not only possessed of a demonstrable unity of structure, which renders its

fragmentary origin inconceivable, but there are throughout manifest allusions from one part to another, one section either referring in express terms to what is contained in others, or implying their existence, being based upon those that precede and unintelligible without them, and presupposing those that follow. The minute examinations to which this very hypothesis has driven the friends of truth have shown that such explicit or tacit allusions are traceable everywhere; and wherever they occur they make it clear that the writer must have been cognizant of the paragraphs alluded to, and have felt at liberty to assume that his readers were acquainted with them likewise. Of course this is quite inconsistent with the notion that each of these paragraphs came from a different source, and was written independently of the rest.

It was refuted by Ewald[1] in his earliest publication, which still deserves careful study, and still more thoroughly by F. H. Ranke.[2]

SUPPLEMENT HYPOTHESIS.

Repelled by the inconsistencies and incongruities of the Fragment Hypothesis, Bleek, Tuch, Stähelin, De Wette, Knobel[3] and others advocated what is known as

[1] Die Composition der Genesis kritisch Untersucht, von Dr. H. Á. Ewald, 1823.

[2] Untersuchungen über den Pentateuch, von Dr. Friedrich Heinrich Ranke, Pfarrer. Vol. i., 1834; Vol. ii., 1840.

[3] The matured views of Bleek are given in the posthumous publication, Einleitung in das Alte Testament, 1860. In his opinion, "after Ex. vi. 2-8, the determination of Elohistic constituents, if not impossible, is incomparably more difficult and uncertain than in the preceding history." 4th Edit., p. 92. He maintained that there was much in the Pentateuch that was genuinely Mosaic, and especially that many of the laws proceeded from Moses in the form in which they are there preserved, and were committed to writing by Moses himself, or at least in

the Supplement Hypothesis. This is a modification of the Documentary, not on the side of a still further and indefinite division, but on the opposite side of a closer union. It was consequently a reaction in the right direction; a confession that what had been sundered without limit, as though its several parts were void of all coherence, really do belong together; it is an admission, so far as it goes, of the cogency of the arguments, by which the various parts of the Pentateuch can be shown to be linked together.

The Supplement Hypothesis retained the Elohist and the Jehovist of the older theory; but, instead of making them the authors of distinct and independent documents, which were subsequently combined and pieced together by a different hand, it supposed that the Elohist first prepared his treatise, which lies at the basis throughout of the Pentateuch, and constitutes its groundwork. The Jehovist, who lived later, undertook to prepare an enlarged edition of this older history. He accordingly retained all that was in the earlier work, preserving its form and language, only introducing into it and incor-

the Mosaic age. Kommentar über die Genesis, von Dr. Friedrich Tuch, 1838. Kritische Untersuchungen über den Pentateuch, die Bücher Josua, Richter, Samuels und der Könige, von J. J. Stähelin, 1843. Stähelin is peculiar in beginning his literary analysis with the laws, and then applying the results to the historical portions of the Pentateuch and the Book of Joshua. De Wette, who at first seemed to waver between the Fragment and Document Hypothesis, finally fell in with the supplementary view. His latest views are given in the sixth edition of his Lehrbuch der Historisch-kritischen Einleitung, 1845. Die Genesis erklärt von August Knobel, 1852. This was followed in succession by commentaries on the remaining books of the Pentateuch and on Joshua. Knobel endeavored to remove the difficulty arising from the large number of passages in which the characteristics of the Elohist and Jehovist were blended, by assuming that they belonged to the Jehovist, who in them drew from two antecedent sources, which he denominated the Rechtsbuch and the Kriegsbuch. It is the same difficulty that Hupfeld sought to relieve by his assumption of a second Elohist.

porating with it sections of his own, supplying omissions, and amplifying what needed to be more fully stated, thus supplementing it by means of such materials as were within his reach, and making such additions as he esteemed important.

This form of the hypothesis not only provides, as the old document theory had done, for those evidences of unity which bind the various Elohim passages to one another, and also the various Jehovah passages. But it accounts still further for the fact, inexplicable on the document theory, that the Jehovah sections are related to the Elohim sections, presuppose them, or contain direct and explicit allusions to them. This is readily explained by the Supplement Hypothesis ; for not only would the Elohist and Jehovist be aware of what they had respectively written, or of what they intended to write in the course of their work, but in addition the Jehovist is supposed to have the treatise of the Elohist in his hands, to which all that he writes himself is merely supplemental. It is quite natural for him, therefore, to make allusions to what the Elohist had written. But it is not so easy to account for the fact, which is also of repeated occurrence, that the Elohim passages allude to or presuppose the contents of Jehovah passages. Here the theory signally breaks down. For by the hypothesis the Elohist wrote first an independent production, without any knowledge of, and, of course, without the possibility of making any reference to the additions which the Jehovist was subsequently to make.

Another halting-place in this hypothesis was the impossibility of making out any consistent view of the relation in which the Jehovist stood to the antecedent labors of the Elohist. The great proof, which was insisted upon, of the existence of the Jehovist as distinct from the Elohist, and supplementing the treatise of the latter, lay in the diversity of style and thought which are alleged to characterize these two classes of sections respectively. Hence it was necessary to assume that the Jehovist faithfully retained the language of the Elohim document unaltered, and that his own peculiarities were limited to the sections which he introduced himself, and that there they were exhibited freely and without reserve. It is frequently the case, however, that the ideas or diction which have been represented to belong to one of these classes of sections are found likewise in the other class. Thus, Elohim passages are found to contain those words and phrases which have been alleged to characterize the Jehovist, and to contain ideas and statements which are said to be peculiarly Jehovistic. Here it is necessary to affirm that the Jehovist, instead of faithfully transcribing the Elohim document, has altered its language and inserted expressions or ideas of his own. Again, Jehovah passages are found in which those characteristics of style and thought appear which are elsewhere claimed as peculiar to the Elohist. This is explained by saying that the Jehovist in such cases has imitated the style or adopted the ideas of the Elohist, and has sought to make his own additions conform as far as possible to the characteristic style of the work which he is supplementing. Again, while it is alleged that the Elohim and Jehovah passages are for the most part clearly distinguishable, there are instances in which it is difficult, if not impossible, to draw a sharp line of demarcation between contiguous Elohim and Jehovah passages, and to determine precisely where one ends and the other begins. Here the Jehovist is thought to have used art to cover up his additions. He has fitted them with such care and skill to the work of his predecessor that the point of junction cannot be discerned, and it has been made to look like one continuous composition. Instead of allowing, as in other instances, his insertions to remain visibly distinct from the original document, he has acted as if he desired to confuse his additions with the pre-existing work, and to make their separation impossible.

Now, apart from the fact that these attempted explanations of phenomena at variance with the primary hypothesis are merely shifts and subterfuges to evade the difficulty which they create, and that this is bringing unproved hypotheses to support a hypothesis, every fresh addition making the superstructure weaker instead of confirming it, the view which is thus presented of the Jehovist is inconsistent with itself. At one time we must suppose him to allow the most obvious diversity of style and ideas between the Elohist sections and his own without the slightest concern or any attempt at producing conformity; at others he modifies the language of the Elohist, or carefully copies him in the sections which he adds himself in order to effect this conformity, though no special motive can be assigned for this difference in his conduct. He sometimes leaves his additions unconnected with the original work which he is supplementing; at other times he weaves them in so adroitly as to create the appearance of continuity, and this again without any assignable motive. A hypothetical personage, who has to be represented by turns as artless and artful, as an honest reporter and a designing interpolator, as skilful and a bungler, as greatly concerned about a conformity of style and thought in some passages, of which he is wholly regardless in others, and of whose existence we have no other evidence than that afforded by these contradictory allegations respecting him, can scarcely be said to have his reality established thus. And a hypothesis which is reduced to the necessity of bolstering itself up in this way has not yet reached firm footing.

Kurtz furnished the best refutation in detail of the critical analysis adopted by the advocates of the Supplement Hypothesis. The unity and Mosaic authorship of Genesis were also ably defended by Drechsler, and that of the entire Pentateuch by Hävernick and Keil. The most complete thesaurus in reply to objections is that of Hengstenberg, upon whom Welte is largely dependent.[1]

CRYSTALLIZATION HYPOTHESIS.

The simplicity of the Supplement Hypothesis, which was its chief recommendation, proved inadequate to relieve the complications which beset the path of the divisive critics. Attempts to remedy these inconveniences were accordingly made in different lines by Ewald and by Hupfeld, both of whom, but particularly the latter, contributed to smooth the way for their successors. Ewald's maiden publication, in 1823, was directed against the extreme disintegration of the Fragment Hypothesis.

---

[1] Beiträge zur Vertheidigung und Begründung der Einheit des Pentateuches, von Joh. Heinr. Kurtz, Erster Beitrag, Nachweis der Einheit von Gen. i.–iv., 1844. This preliminary essay was followed in 1846 by his complete and masterly treatise Die Einheit der Genesis. Unfortunately Kurtz was subsequently induced to yield the position, which he had so successfully maintained, in his Geschichte des Alten Bundes, and to admit that the Pentateuch did not receive its final form until the generation succeeding that of Moses. Die Einheit und Aechtheit der Genesis von Dr. Moritz Drechsler, 1838. Handbuch der historisch-kritischen Einleitung in das Alte Testament, von H. A. Ch. Hävernick, Part I., Section 2, 1837. Lehrbuch der historisch-kritischen Einleitung in die kanonischen Schriften des Alten Testamentes, von Karl Friedrich Keil, 1853. Die Authentie des Pentateuches erwiesen von Ernst Wilhelm Hengstenberg, vol. i., 1836 ; vol. ii., 1839. Nachmosaisches im Pentateuch, beleuchtet von Dr. Benedikt Welte, 1841. Also his important additions and corrections to Herbst's Einleitung, which he edited, and of which the first division of the second part, containing the Introduction to the Pentateuch, appeared in 1842.

6

His own scheme, proposed twenty years later,[1] has been appropriately called the Crystallization Hypothesis. This is a modification of the Supplementary by increasing the number engaged in supplementing from one to a series successively operating at distinct periods. The nucleus, or most ancient portion of the Pentateuch, in his opinion, consisted of the remnants of four primitive treatises now existing only in fragments embedded in the various strata which were subsequently accumulated around them. This was followed in the second place by what he calls the Book of the Origins, and this by what he denominates the third, fourth, and fifth prophetic narrators, each of whom in succession added his accretion to what had been previously recorded, and the last of whom worked over all that preceded, together with his own additions and alterations, into one continuous work. Then the Deuteronomist wrote Deuteronomy, which was first issued as an independent publication, but was subsequently incorporated with the work of his predecessors. And thus the Pentateuch, or rather the Hexateuch, for the Pentateuch and Joshua were regarded by him, as by the majority of advanced modern critics generally, as one work—thus the Hexateuch slowly grew to its present dimensions, a vast conglomerate, including these various accessions made in the course of many centuries.

MODIFIED DOCUMENT HYPOTHESIS.

Hupfeld[2] undertook to remove the obstacles, which blocked the way of the Supplement Hypothesis, in a

[1] Heinrich Ewald, Geschichte des Volkes Israel bis Christus, vol. i., p. 60 sqq. 1843.

[2] Die Quellen der Genesis und die Art ihrer Zusammensetzung von neuem untersucht, von D. Hermann Hupfeld, 1853. The existence of a second Elohist had been maintained long before, and a partition made

different manner; not by introducing fresh supplements, but by abandoning the supplementing process altogether, and falling back upon the Document Hypothesis, of which he proposed an important modification. He aimed chiefly to establish two things : First, that the Jehovist sections were not disconnected additions to a pre-existing document, but possessed a continuity and independence, which shows that they must have constituted a separately existing document. In order to this he attempted to bridge over the breaks and chasms by the aid of scattered clauses arbitrarily sundered from their context in intervening Elohim sections, and thus made a shift to preserve a scanty semblance of continuity. In the second place, he maintained the composite character of the Elohist sections, and that they constituted not one but two documents. The troublesome passages, which corresponded neither with the characteristics of the Elohist nor the Jehovist, but appeared to combine them both, were alleged to be the product of a third writer, who while he used the name Elohim had the diction and other peculiarities of the Jehovist, and whom he accordingly called the second Elohist. Upon this scheme there were three independent documents; that of the first Elohist, the second Elohist, and the Jehovist. And these were put together in their present form by a redactor who allowed himself the liberty of inserting, retrenching,

on this basis by Ilgen in Die Urkunden des ersten Buchs von Moses in ihrer Urgestalt, 1798 ; but it met no approval at the time. Eduard Boehmer, in Das Erste Buch der Thora, adopted the scheme of Hupfeld, though differing materially in many points in the details of the analysis. E. Schrader, in editing the eighth edition of De Wette's Introduction, in 1869, follows the same general scheme, with some modifications of the analysis. He designates the authors of the documents as the Annalistic, the Theocratic, and the Prophetic Narrators, corresponding severally to the first and second Elohists and the Jehovist of Hupfeld's nomenclature.

modifying, transposing, and combining at his own pleasure. All references from one document to the contents of another, and in general any phenomena that conflict with the requirements of the hypothesis, are ascribed to the redactor.

There are several halting-places in this scheme of Hupfeld. (1) One is that the creation of a second Elohist destroys the continuity and completeness of the first. The second Elohist is supposed to begin abruptly with the twentieth chapter of Genesis. From that point onward to the end of the book, with the exception of ch. xxiii. which records the death and burial of Sarah, the great body of the Elohim passages are given to the second Elohist, and nothing reserved for the first but occasional disconnected scraps, which never could have formed a separate and independent record, and which, moreover, are linked with and imply much that is assigned to the other documents. So that it is necessary to assume that this document once contained the very matter which has been sundered from it. These scattered points simply outline the history, apart from which they have no value and no meaning. Severed from the body of the narrative to which they are attached they are an empty frame without contents. This frame only exists for the sake of the historical material, to which it is adjusted and indissolubly belongs.

(2) It is also a suspicious circumstance that the first Elohist breaks off almost entirely so near the point where the second Elohist begins. All Elohist passages before Gen. xx. are given to the first Elohist; all after that, with trifling exceptions, to the second Elohist. This looks more like the severance of what was once continuous, than the disentangling of documents once separate which the redactor had worked together section by section in compiling his history.

(3) Another suspicious circumstance is the intricate manner in which the Jehovist and second Elohist are thought to be combined. In many passages they are so intimately blended that they cannot be separated. And in general it is admitted to be impossible to establish any clearly defined criteria of language, style, or thought between them. This has the appearance of a factitious division of what is really the product of a single writer. There is no reason of any moment, whether in the diction or in the matter, for assuming that the Jehovist and the second Elohist were distinct writers.

(4) It is indeed claimed that the first Elohist is clearly distinguishable in diction and in matter from the Jehovist and the second Elohist. But there are several considerations which quite destroy the force of the argument for distinct documents from this source. *a.* If the Elohim sections prior to Gen. xx. are thought to have a diction different from that of the Jehovist; and the great body of the Elohim sections after Gen. xx. have a diction confessedly indistinguishable from that of the Jehovist, the presumption certainly is that the difference alleged in the early chapters rests on too limited an induction; and when the induction is carried further, it appears that the conclusion has been too hasty, and that no real difference exists. *b.* Again, the great bulk of the narrative of Genesis, so far as it concerns transactions in ordinary life, is divided between the Jehovist and the second Elohist. The first Elohist is limited to genealogies, legal sections, extraordinary events, such as the creation and flood, or mere isolated notices, as of births, deaths, ages, migrations, etc. That matter of a different description should call for the use of a different set of words, while in matter of the same sort like words are used is just what might be expected ; and there is no need of assuming different documents in

order to account for it. *c.* Still further, when, as in Gen.
xxxiv., a narrative is for special reasons assigned in part
to the first Elohist, it is as impossible to distinguish its
diction from that of the other documents as it elsewhere
is to distinguish the diction of the second Elohist from
that of the Jehovist; and other grounds of distinction
must be resorted to in order to effect a separation. All
this makes it evident that the variant diction alleged is
due to the difference in the matter and not to diversity
of documents.

(5) The function assigned to the redactor assumes
that he acts in the most capricious and inconsistent
manner, more so even than the Jehovist of the Supplement Hypothesis. At times he is represented as scrupulously careful to preserve everything contained in his
various sources, though it leads to needless and unmeaning repetition; at others he omits large and important
sections, though the document from which they are
dropped is thus reduced to a mutilated remnant. Where
his sources disagree he sometimes retains the narrative
of each unchanged, thus placing the whole case fairly
before his readers; at others he alters them into correspondence, which is hardly consistent with historical
honesty. Variant narratives of the same event are sometimes harmonized by combining them, thus confusing
both; sometimes they are mistaken for distinct and even
widely separated events and related as such, an error
which reflects upon his intelligence, since critics with
the incomplete data which he has left them are able to
correct it. He sometimes reproduces his sources just as
he finds them; at others he alters their whole complexion by freely manipulating the text or making additions of his own. Everything in diction, style, or ideas
which is at variance with the requirements of the hypothesis, is laid to his account, and held to be due to his

interference. The present text does not suit the hypothesis, therefore it must have been altered, and the redactor must have done it.

It is evident how convenient it is to have a redactor always at hand to whom every miscarriage of the hypothesis can be attributed. But it is also evident that the frequent necessity for invoking his aid seriously weakens the cause which he is summoned to support. It is further evident that the suspicions cast upon the accuracy with which the redactor has transmitted the various texts which he had before him undermines the entire basis of the hypothesis. For it undertakes to establish the existence of the so-called documents, and to discriminate between them, by verbal criteria, which are nullified if the original texts have been tampered with. And it is still further evident that the opposite traits of character impliedly ascribed to the redactor, the utterly capricious and irrational conduct imputed to him, and the wanton and aimless manipulation of his authorities, for which no motive can be imagined, tend to make this most important functionary an impossible conception.

Both Ewald and Hupfeld were regarded at the time as having made a retrograde movement instead of an advance, by falling back from the simplicity of the then dominant Supplement Hypothesis into a greater complexity than that of the original Document Hypothesis. The fact is, however, that the complexity inevitably grows, as the critics aim at greater precision, and endeavor to adapt their scheme more exactly to the phenomena with which they have to deal. The multiplication of machinery, which is necessary before all can work smoothly, so overloads their apparatus that it is in danger of breaking down by its own weight. They find themselves obliged to pile hypothesis upon hypothesis in order to relieve difficulties, and explain diversities, and account for irregularities by subdivided documents, and successive recensions, and a series of redactors, and unfathered glosses, and variegated legal strata, and diaskeuasts in unlimited profusion, until the whole thing reaches a state of confusion worse confounded, almost equivalent to that of the exploded Fragment Hypothesis itself.

For the sake of brevity the Pentateuchal documents are commonly denoted by symbols. Dr. Dillmann employs the first four letters of the alphabet for the purpose; he calls the Elohist A, the second Elohist B, the Jehovist C, and the Deuteronomist D. Others use the same symbols, but change the order of their application. In the nomenclature that is now most prevalent the term Elohist is applied exclusively to what used to be known as the second Elohist, and it is represented by E; the Jehovist by J. J and E are alleged to have emanated from prophetic circles, J in the southern kingdom of Judah, and E in the northern kingdom of Israel. The second Elohist having been separated from what used to be known as the Elohist document, the remnant was by Wellhausen fancifully called Q, the initial of quattuor = 4, because of the four covenants which it contains. Others prefer to designate it as P, the priestly writing, in distinction from the prophetic histories J and E. The critics further distinguish J^1 and J^2, E^1 and E^2, P^1, P^2 and P^3, D^1 and D^2, which represent different strata in these documents. Different Redactors are embraced under the general symbol R, viz., Rj who combined J and E, Rd who added D to JE, and Rh who completed the Hexateuch by combining P with JED.

THE GROUNDS OF LITERARY PARTITION CONSIDERED.

While these various hypotheses, which have thus arisen each on the ruins of its predecessor, are, as has been

shown, individually encumbered with insuperable difficulties peculiar to each, the common arguments by which
their advocates seek to establish them are insufficient
and inconclusive.

1. The first argument, as already stated, in defence of
these several partition hypotheses, is drawn from the
alternate employment of the divine names Elohim and
Jehovah. It may be observed, however, that so far as
there is any thing remarkable in the alternation of these
names in the Pentateuch, it is confined almost entirely to
the book of Genesis, and chiefly to the earlier portions
of that book. It cannot, of course, be maintained that
the same writer could not make use of both names.
They are intermingled in various proportions in almost
every book of the Bible. The occurrence of both in the
same composition can of itself create no suspicion of its
lack of unity. The special grounds which are relied
upon in this case are, (1) the regularity of their alternation in successive sections; and (2) the testimony of
Ex. vi. 3, which is understood to declare that the name
Jehovah is not pre-Mosaic and was not in use in the
days of the patriarchs, whence it is inferred that P, by
whom this is recorded, systematically avoided the use of
Jehovah prior to the time when God thus revealed himself to Moses.

As to the first of these points, remarkable as is the
alternation of the divine names, particularly in the earlier
chapters of Genesis, it does not coincide so precisely
with sections or paragraphs as the advocates of these
hypotheses would have us imagine; for with all the care
that they have taken in dividing these sections to suit
their theory, each of these names is found repeatedly in
sections mainly characterized by the other. The divergence between the hypothesis and the facts, on which it
is professedly based, is so great that it cannot give a

satisfactory explanation of them; and the arbitrary methods to which its advocates are forced to resort, in order to remove this divergence, are absolutely destructive of the hypothesis itself, as can be readily shown.

For the critics are obliged to play fast and loose with the text in a manner and to a degree which renders all their reasoning precarious. The alternation of the divine names Elohim and Jehovah is made by them the key of their whole position. This is the starting-point of the partition, and of the entire hypothesis of the separate documents. All the other criteria are supplementary to this; they are worked out on this basis, and find in it whatever justification and proof of their validity they have. All hinges ultimately, therefore, on the exact transmission of these fundamental and determining words. At the outset the lines of demarcation are run exclusively by them; and an error in these initial lines, by confusing the limits of the documents, would introduce error into their respective criteria as deduced from the inspection of these faulty passages. If there is anything that must be absolutely fixed and resolutely adhered to, if the document hypothesis is to stand, it is the accuracy of these divine names, which are the pillars on which the whole critical structure rests. And yet the critics, in repeated instances, declare them to be incorrect or out of place. They are, in fact, forced by the perplexities of their situation thus to cut away the ground from beneath their own feet. The divine names are made the prime criteria for distinguishing the so-called documents. It is said that J (the Jehovist) characteristically uses Jehovah, E (the Elohist) Elohim, and P (the priestly writer) Elohim as far as Ex. vi. 2, 3, and Jehovah thereafter. But the trouble is that with their utmost efforts the critics find it impossible to adjust the documents into conformity with this proposed scheme; though their alleged correspondence with it is the sole ultimate warrant for their existence, the supreme criterion, on which all other criteria depend. In the first place, Elohim is repeatedly found along with Jehovah in sections attributed to J. Here the critics explain that the author of this document used both names as the occasion demanded. But this is putting the use of these names on an entirely different ground from that of the distinctive usage of separate writers. If J could use both of these names, and in so doing was governed by their inherent signification and by the appropriateness of each to the connection in which they are severally employed, why might not P and E do the same? or why, in fact, is there any need for J, P, or E, or for any other than the one author to whom a uniform and well-accredited tradition attributes all that it has been proposed to parcel among these unknown and undiscoverable personages? The appropriate use of these divine names, as ascertained from the acknowledged employment of them by J, taken in connection with the explicit statement of Ex. vi. 3, not in the perverted sense put upon it by the critics, but in its true signification, as determined by the numerous parallels in the book of Exodus, and throughout the entire Old Testament, will explain their alternation in Genesis in a satisfactory manner, which the hypothetical documents have not done, and cannot do.

Again, Jehovah occurs repeatedly in sections attributed to P and E, where, by the hypothesis, only Elohim should be found. Every possible evasion is employed to get rid of these unwelcome facts. Where the facts are at variance with the hypothesis, the invariable assumption is that the hypothesis is right and the facts are wrong, and require correction. The redactor has for some unimaginable reason been at fault. He has inserted a verse, or a clause, or simply the unsuitable divine name of his own motion, without there being anything in the original text that corresponded to it ; or he has erased the divine name that was in the text, and substituted another for it ; or he has mixed two texts by inserting into the body of one document a clause supposed to be taken from another. And thus the attempt is made to bolster up the hypothesis by an inference drawn from the hypothesis. And the effect is to unsettle the text at those crucial points where accuracy and certainty are essential to the validity of the hypothesis, not to speak of the corollaries deducible from it.

Elohim occurs inconveniently for the critics in Gen. vii. 9 ; hence Kautzsch claims that it must have been originally Jehovah, while Dillmann insists that vs. 8, 9 were inserted by R (the redactor). The critics wish to make it appear that two accounts of the flood, by P and J respectively, have been blended in the existing text ; and that vs. 7–9 is J's account, and vs. 13–16 that by P. But unfortunately for them, this is blocked by the occurrence in each one of the verses assigned to J, of expressions foreign to J and peculiar to P ; and to cap the climax, the divine name is not J's but P's. The repetition cannot, therefore, be wrested into an indication of a duplicate narrative, but simply, as its language clearly shows, emphasizes the fact that the entry into the ark was made on the self-same day that the flood began.

"And Jehovah shut him in" (vii. 16b), occurs in the midst of a P paragraph ; hence it is alleged that this solitary clause has been inserted from a supposed parallel narrative by J. But this overlooks the significant and evidently intended contrast of the two divine names in this verse, a significance to which Delitzsch calls attention, thus discrediting the basis of the critical analysis, which he nevertheless accepts. Animals of every species went into the ark, as Elohim, the God of creation and

providence directed, mindful of the preservation of what
he had made ; Jehovah, the guardian of his people, shut
Noah in.

In xiv. 22, Jehovah occurs not in a J section, and is
declared spurious for that reason ; though it is the name
of God as known to Abram, in distinction from him as
he was known to Melchizedek (ver. 19).

Ch. xvii. is assigned to P because of the exclusive use
of Elohim in it after ver. 1 ; hence it is claimed that Jehovah in ver. 1 is an error for Elohim, notwithstanding
the regular recurrence of Jehovah in all that preceded
since the call of Abram (xii. 1), the identity of the phrase
with xii. 7 ; xviii. 1, and the obvious requirements of this
passage. Jehovah, the God of Abram, here reveals himself as God Almighty and Elohim, to signalize his power
to accomplish what nature could not effect, and to pledge
the immediate fulfilment of the long-delayed promise.

Ch. xx. records the affair with Abimelech, and the
name of God is for this reason Elohim, until the last
verse, where Jehovah's interference for the protection of
Sarah is spoken of. The significance of this change of
names is lost upon the critics, who assign the chapter to
E because of Elohim, and then can account for Jehovah
in no other way than by imputing ver. 18 to R.

In xxi. 1, 2, there is a curious specimen of critical dissection. Each verse is split in two, and one sentence
fashioned out of the two first halves, and another out of
the two second halves. The critical necessity for this
grows out of the need of finding the birth of Isaac in
both J and P. The alleged equivalence of the two
clauses in ver. 1 is made a pretext for sundering them,
and assigning to J " And Jehovah visited Sarah, as he
had said ; " and to P the rest of the verse, " And Jehovah
did unto Sarah as he had spoken," which last is then
filled out by ver. 2b, " at the set time of which Elohim

had spoken to him." But as it is inadmissible for Jehovah
to stand in a P clause (ver. 1b), it is assumed that it must
originally have been Elohim. This is all built upon the
sand, however; for ver. 1 does not contain two identical
statements. The second is an advance upon the first,
stating that the purpose of the visitation was to fulfil a
promise; and what that promise was is further stated
in ver. 2. All is closely connected and progressive
throughout; and it cannot be rent asunder as the critics
propose. Jehovah, the God of Abraham, visited Sarah,
and fulfilled his word to her, and Sarah bare her son at
the set time that Elohim, the mighty Creator, had said.
The names are in every way appropriate as they stand.[1]

In Abimelech's interview with Abraham, resulting in
the naming of Beersheba, the name of God is appropriately Elohim (xxi. 22, 23); but when Abraham worshipped there he called, with equal propriety, on the
name of Jehovah (ver. 33). The critics, ignoring the true
reason of the interchange of names, tell us that ver. 33 is
a fragment of J inserted by R in a narrative of E.

In ch. xxii. Elohim puts Abraham to the trial, the angel of Jehovah interposes and blesses him. The demand of the Creator for the surrender of the dearest and
the best is supplemented by the God of grace and salvation, who approves and rewards the mental surrender,
and in the substituted animal supplies for the time then
present an accepted type of the true sacrifice. This obviously designed and significant change of names is lost
upon the critics, who find only the unmeaning usage of
distinct writers, and can only account for Moriah,[2] (ver.

---

[1] Kautsch seems to be alone in venturing to split xxxix. 3 and 5, in a
similar manner, and giving the second clause in each verse to E, with
its Jehovah converted into Elohim.

[2] A compound proper name with an abbreviated form of Jehovah as
one of its constituents.

2), or Jehovah (ver. 11), as textual errors, and for the repeated occurrence of Jehovah subsequently by making
vs. 14–18, an interpolation by R, or an insertion from J.
But the alleged interpolation is plainly an essential part
of the narrative ; the story of such a trial, so borne, is
pointless without the words of commendation and blessing.

Isaac's blessing of Esau (xxvii. 27, 28) is torn asunder
because Jehovah in the first sentence is followed by Elohim in the second.

So Jacob's dream, in which he beholds the angels of
Elohim (xxviii. 12), and Jehovah (ver. 13) ; although his
waking (ver. 16) from the sleep into which he had fallen
(vs. 11, 12) shows that these cannot be parted. Jacob's
vow (vs. 20, 21) is arbitrarily amended by striking out
" then shall Jehovah be my God," because of his previous
mention of Elohim when referring to his general providential benefits.

The story of the birth of Leah's first four sons (xxix.
31–35), and that of the fifth and sixth (xxx. 17–20), are
traced to different documents notwithstanding their
manifest connection, because Jehovah occurs in the
former and Elohim in the latter.

Elohim in xxxi. 50, in a so-called J paragraph, is for
that reason summarily pronounced spurious.

Since Elohim occurs in xxxiii. 5b, 11, these are declared to be isolated clauses from E in a J section.

The battle with Amalek (Ex. xvii. 8–13) is assigned to
E because of Elohim, ver. 9 ; but the direction to record
it, the commemorative altar, and the oath of perpetual
hostility to Amalek (vs. 14–16), which stand in a most intimate relation to it, are held to be from another document, because of Jehovah.

In Jethro's visit (Ex. xviii.) Elohim (eleven times)
naturally preponderates in what is said by or to one not

of the chosen race ; and yet Jehovah is used (six times)
where there is specific allusion to the God of Israel.
But each Jehovah clause must, according to the critics,
have been inserted in E's narrative by R from an assumed parallel account by J.

Ex. xix. is mainly referred to E ; but the repeated occurrence of Jehovah compels the critics to assume that
R has in several instances substituted it for Elohim, and
even made more serious changes in the text.

Ex. xxiv. is divided between E and J ; but the division
cannot be so made as to correspond with the divine
names in the current text.

No critic pretends to follow the indication of the divine names in dissecting Ex. xxxii.

Dr. Harper, in the "Hebraica," vi. 1, p. 35, says of the
critical analysis of Ex. i. 1–vii. 7, " the language is but
a poor guide, owing probably to R's interference ; not
even the names of the Deity are to be relied on implicitly, being freely intermingled." And p. 47, on Ex. vii.
8–xii. 51 : " In this section the name of the Deity is exclusively Jehovah, which must have been substituted by
R in all the E passages." In the "Hebraica," vi. 4, p. 269,
he confesses that Jehovah runs " all through E's material "
in the section Num. x. 29–xvii. 28 (E. V. ver. 13) ; and p.
287 complains in regard to Num. xx. 1–xxvii. 11, of "the
unsatisfactory use of the names of the Deity ; Yahweh is
the prevailing name, Elohim occurring but nine times in
the entire section ; this is, however, more easily explained
on the R hypothesis than by any other." That is to say,
the use of the divine names runs athwart the critical hypothesis to such an extent as to be quite unsatisfactory to
its advocates. And the easiest way out of the difficulty is
to assume that R has altered the name wherever the
exigencies of the hypothesis require such a supposition.

For the striking significance of the divine names in the

history of Balaam (Num. xxii.–xxiv.) the critics have no
appreciation, but seek to resolve all by their mechanical
rule of blended documents. The occurrence of Elohim
four times in xxii. 2–21 is urged as determining it to
belong to E; but Jehovah also occurs four times, where
it is assumed that the word was originally Elohim, but it
has been changed by R. Jehovah predominates in vs.
22–35 J, but Elohim is found in ver. 22, for which R is
again held responsible. The next two chapters are divided between the same two documents, but with some
uncertainty to which each should belong. Wellhausen
assigns ch. xxiii. to J, and ch. xxiv. to E; Dillmann re-
verses it, giving ch. xxiii. to E, and ch. xxiv. to J. But
however they dispose of them, the divine names will not
suit, and R must be supposed to have manipulated them
here again.

The real facts are these. Balaam only once uses Elohim (xxii. 38); and then it is to mark the contrast between the divine and the merely human. Apart from
this he invariably uses the divine name Jehovah, whether
he is speaking to Balak's messengers (xxii. 8, 13, 18, 19),
to Balak (xxiii. 3, 12, 26; xxiv. 13), or uttering his prophecies (xxiii. 8, 21; xxiv. 6). He thus indicates that it was
Jehovah whom he professed to consult, and whose will he
undertook to declare. And it was because of his supposed power with the God of Israel that Balak desired
his aid. Hence Balak uses Jehovah in addressing
Balaam (xxiii. 17; xxiv. 11); only once Elohim (xxiii. 27),
as non-Israelites commonly do. When the writer speaks
of God in connection with this heathen seer, he steadfastly uses Elohim at the outset. Balaam regularly proposes to tell the messengers of Balak what Jehovah will
say to him, but the writer with equal uniformity says
that Elohim came to him, and spoke to him (xxii. 9, 10,
12, 20, 22). He is not recognized as an accredited prophet

7

of Jehovah. But while it is only Elohim, the general term denoting the Deity, which is put by the sacred writer in relation to Balaam considered as a heathen seer, it is the Angel of Jehovah who comes forth to confront him on his unhallowed errand, and Jehovah the guardian and defender of Israel who constrains him to pronounce a blessing instead of a curse. Hence from xxii. 22 onward, wherever the writer speaks, he uses the name Jehovah, not only in the encounter by the way but after his arrival, as determining what he shall say. To this there are but two exceptions. In xxiii. 4, when Balaam had gone to look for auguries, " Elohim met him," reminding us that he was but a heathen seer still; yet it was Jehovah (vs. 5, 16) who put the word in his mouth. In xxiv. 2, " the Spirit of Elohim came upon him," expresses the thought that he was divinely inspired, and spoke by an impulse from above and not from promptings of his own ; but his conviction that it was Jehovah's purpose to bless Israel kept him from seeking auguries as at other times (ver. 1). The partition hypothesis obliterates this nice discrimination entirely, and sees nothing but the unmeaning usage of different writers coupled with R's arbitrary disturbance of the text for no imaginable reason.

This rapid survey of a few prominent passages sufficiently shows the character of the evasions by which the critics seek to cover up the lack of correspondence between their hypotheses and the textual phenomena of the divine names. This want of correspondence betrays itself in numerous signal instances. The attempts to relieve it are based on arbitrary assumptions, which are mere inferences from the hypothesis which they are adduced to support. In this process passages which are inseparable are rent asunder, and in many cases the real significance of the divine names is ignored or marred.

And as a further consequence the main point above insisted upon is fully established. The current hypothesis of the critics is built on minute verbal distinctions, which imply an accuracy and certainty of text which they themselves unsettle by their frequent assumptions of errors and of manipulations by the redactor. If he altered the divine names, and inserted or modified clauses containing them in the instances and to the extent alleged, who is to vouch that he has been more scrupulous elsewhere? The hypothesis is self-destructive; for it can only be defended by arguments which undermine its foundations. And even if it were not possible, as in fact it is, to account satisfactorily for the interchange of divine names on other grounds, the proof is ample that the hypothesis of distinct writers will not explain it.

Here, however, the testimony of Ex. vi. 2, 3, is adduced to show that P carefully and designedly avoided the use of the name Jehovah in all that he had previously written, but regularly employed this name from that place onward. The passage reads : " God spake unto Moses, and said unto him, I am Jehovah : and I appeared unto Abraham, unto Isaac, and unto Jacob as God Almighty ; but by my name Jehovah I was not known unto them." The critics interpret this to mean that the name Jehovah was then first revealed to Moses, and that it had not been in use in the time of the patriarchs. They hence regard all prior sections containing the name Jehovah as in conflict with this statement, especially as Jehovah is used not only in the language of the writer himself, but when he is reporting the words of those who lived long before Moses's time. Such sections, it is said, imply a different belief as to the origin and use of this sacred name, and must, therefore, be attributed to another writer, who held that it was known from the earliest periods, and who has recorded his idea upon that subject (Gen. iv. 26) that men began to call upon the name of Jehovah in the days of Enosh.

But the sense thus put upon Ex. vi. 3, is altogether inadmissible. For

(1) It is plain, upon the critics' own hypothesis, that the redactor, to whom in their view the Pentateuch and Genesis owe their present form, did not so understand it. After recording the history of the patriarchs, in which free use is made of the name Jehovah, he is here supposed to introduce the statement, from the mouth of God himself, that they had never heard this name, and thus to have stultified himself completely.

(2) It is equally plain that it could not have been so intended by the writer. The statement that God was not known by his name Jehovah unto the patriarchs is explained by the repeated declaration that Israel (Ex. vi. 7; x. 2; xvi. 12; xxix. 46), the Egyptians (vii. 5; xiv. 4, 18), and Pharaoh (vii. 17; viii. 6, 18 (E. V. 10, 22)); ix. 14, 29, comp. v. 2) should know that he was Jehovah; not that they should be told that this was his name, but that they should witness the manifestation of those attributes which the name denoted. That he was not so known by the patriarchs can only mean, therefore, that while tokens of God's almighty power had been vouchsafed to them, no such disclosure had been made of the perfections indicated by his name Jehovah as was now to be granted to their descendants.

(3) The uniform usage of Scripture proves the same thing. A true apprehension of the divine perfections, and not a mere acquaintance with the word Jehovah, is the constant meaning of the phrase " to know the name of Jehovah " (1 Kin. viii. 43; Ps. ix. 11 (E. V. 10); xci. 14; Isa. lii. 6; lxiv. 1 (E. V. 2); Jer. xvi. 21; Ezek. xxxix. 6, 7).

It is important to observe here precisely what these arguments prove, viz., that Ex. vi. 3, was not written with an antiquarian interest, nor from an antiquarian point of view. It does not concern itself about the history of the word Jehovah, and cannot with any fairness be regarded as affirming or denying anything about it. Its sole design is to declare that Jehovah was about to manifest himself in the character represented by this name as he had not done to the patriarchs. Since, then, the writer did not intend to assert that the word was unknown to Abraham, Isaac, and Jacob, there is no reason why, in relating their history, he might not consistently introduce this word in language uttered by them or addressed to them.

Neither, it should also be observed, was the patriarchal history written in the spirit of a verbal antiquary, so as to make a point of rigorously abstaining from employing any word not then in current use. Even if the name Jehovah were not in use prior to the days of Moses, the God of the patriarchs was the very same as Jehovah, and the writer might properly adopt the dialect of his own time in speaking of him for the purpose of asserting the identity of the God of Abraham with the God who appeared to Moses and who led Israel out of Egypt. It is customary to speak of the call of Abraham and of the conversion of Paul, though the patriarch's name was Abram when he was called, and the apostle's name was Saul at the time of his conversion.

Whether the name Jehovah was ante-Mosaic is a legitimate subject of inquiry. But it is not answered categorically in the negative by Ex. vi. 3, nor inferentially in the affirmative by the use of this word in the patriarchal history. That question lay out of the plane of the writer's thoughts in the one place as well as in the other, and no express utterance is made regarding it. Much less have contradictory answers been given to it. The inconsistency which the critics affirm does not exist. There is consequently no difficulty from this source in supposing that the author of Ex. vi. 3, may likewise have penned the Jehovist sections in Genesis. This passage, though one of the pillars of the partition hypothesis, really lends it no support.

Neither does Gen. iv. 26 : "Then began men to call upon the name of Jehovah." This is understood by the critics to affirm that in the belief of J the name Jehovah came into use in the days of Enosh the son of Seth. This might seem to accord with Eve's use of Elohim (iv. 25) at the birth of Seth, and in her conversation with the serpent (iii. 1–5), but does not agree with her mention of Jehovah (iv. 1) at the birth of Cain, long before the time of either Seth or Enosh. Reuss says that the writer here contradicts himself. Dillmann can only evade the difficulty by a transposition of the text. All which simply proves that their interpretation of iv. 26 is false. It fixes the origin not of the word Jehovah, but of the formal invocation of the Most High in public worship.

If we may take a suggestion from Ex. vi. 3, it implies that different names of God have each their distinct and proper signification ; and this inherent signification of the terms must be taken into the account if any successful attempt is to be made to explain their usage. The mechanical and superficial solution of two blended documents offered by the critics will not answer. Ex. vi. 3, instead of contradicting the book of Genesis, affords the key to the phenomena which it presents.

The derivation and primary signification of Elohim are in dispute ; according to some authorities the radical meaning is that of power, according to others it denotes one who is the object of fear and adoration. It is the general name for God, and is applied both to the true God and to pagan deities. Jehovah is not a common but a proper noun. It belongs to the true God alone and is his characteristic name, by which he is distinguished from all others, and by which he made himself known to Israel his chosen people. Accordingly Jehovah denotes specifically what God is in and to Israel; Elohim what he is to other nations as well. That universal agency which is exercised in the world at large, and which is directed upon Israel and Gentiles alike, is, by Elohim, the God of creation and of providence. That special manifestation of himself which is made to his own people is by Jehovah, the God of revelation and of redemption. The sacred writer uses one name or the other according as he contemplates God under one or the other point of view. Where others than those of the chosen race are the speakers, as Abimelech (Gen. xxi. 22, 23) or Pharaoh (xli. 38, 39), it is natural that they should say Elohim, unless they specifically refer to the God of the patriarchs (xxvi. 28), or of Israel (Ex. v. 2), when they will say Jehovah. In transactions between Abraham or his descendants and those of another race God may be spoken of under aspects common to them both, and the name Elohim be employed; or he may be regarded under aspects specifically Israelitish and the name Jehovah be used. Again, as Elohim is the generic name for God as distinguished from beings of a different grade, it is the term proper to be used when God and man, the divine and the human, are contrasted, as Gen. xxx. 2; xxxii. 28; xlv. 5, 7, 8; l. 19, 20.

Hengstenberg [1] maintained that Elohim denotes a lower and Jehovah a higher stage of the knowledge and apprehension of God. The revelation of God advances from his disclosure as Elohim in the creation (Gen. i.) to his disclosure as Jehovah in his covenant with Israel at Sinai; and in the interval between these two extremes he may be designated by one name or the other, according to the conception which is before the mind of the

[1] Die Authentie des Pentateuches, I., p. 286, etc.

writer at the time. In any manifestation surpassing those which have preceded he may be called Jehovah; or if respect is had to more glorious manifestations that are to follow, he may be called Elohim. The names according to this view are relatively employed to indicate higher or lower grades of God's manifestation of himself. There seems to be a measure of truth in this representation of the matter, at least in its general outlines. The name Jehovah shines out conspicuously at three marked epochs, while in the intervals between them it is dimmed and but rarely appears. Jehovah is almost exclusively used in the account of our first parents, recording the initiating of God's kingdom on earth (ch. ii. 4–iv. 16), in its contrast with the material creation described in ch. i.; in the lives of Abraham and Isaac, recording the setting apart of one among the families of mankind to found the chosen people of God in its contrast with the preceding universal degeneracy (Gen. xii.–xvii. 1; xxvi.); and God's revelation of himself to Moses as the deliverer and God of Israel, fulfilling the promises made to their fathers, in contrast with the antecedent period of waiting and foreign residence and oppression. From this time onward Jehovah is the dominant name, since the theocratic relation was then fully established. The general correspondence of Hengstenberg's theory with the marked prevalence of the name Jehovah in the sections indicated, and its comparatively infrequent occurrence in the intervening portions of the history is manifest; but there are exceptional cases, which cannot be accounted for on this sole principle, such as the occasional occurrence of Jehovah in the narrative of the flood, or in the lives of Jacob and Joseph, or of Elohim in Gen. xvii., which is one of the crowning passages in Abraham's life. Here Hengstenberg found himself obliged to resort to unsatisfactory and far-fetched explanations, which have brought

his whole theory into unmerited discredit. These, however, merely show, not that his principle was incorrect,
but that it was partial and was in certain cases limited
by other considerations, which must likewise be taken
into the account in order to a just view of the whole
subject.

Kurtz[1] regards Elohim as denoting almighty power
and Jehovah progressive self-manifestation, which, properly understood and applied, furnishes the needed cor-
rective to the view just considered. For a right conception of the omnipotent energy of Elohim in creation and
providence, and of Jehovah as unfolding, guiding, and
sustaining his scheme of grace, and hence standing in a
special relation to the chosen race and out of relation to
Gentiles, to whom he has not made himself known and
who are suffered to walk in their own ways, supplies the
solution of the exceptional cases above referred to. But
unfortunately Kurtz's antagonism to Hengstenberg pre-
vented his combining his own suggestion with that of
his predecessor. And his fondness for theorizing led
him into unpractical refinements. Thus he explains
Jehovah according to its derivation (Ex. iii. 14) to mean
not the great I AM, the Being by way of eminence, the
self-existent God, the source of all existence, but he who
will become, is ever becoming, the self-developing God,
an expression which taken strictly savors of the pan-
theistic philosophy, for which Kurtz had no affinity,
though in this borrowing its terminology. He further
explains Elohim to be the God of the beginning and of
the end, and Jehovah the God of all that intervenes
between these two extremes. Elohim is the creator and
originator, imparting the initial potency, Jehovah con-
ducts the development, and Elohim is the final judge
whether the development has miscarried through the

[1] Einheit der Genesis, p. xlix. sqq. ; see also p. xxxi., note.

abuse of human freedom, or has reached its proper end so that God is all in all. This might account for the predominance of Elohim in the flood which overwhelmed the guilty world; but it was Jehovah who overthrew the flagitious cities of Sodom and Gomorrah, and swept their abominations from the holy land.

It should further be observed that while in certain cases one of the divine names is manifestly appropriate to the exclusion of the other, there are others in which either name might properly be used, and it is at the discretion of the writer which he will employ. When an event is capable of being viewed under a double aspect, either as belonging to the general scheme of God's universal providence or as embraced within the administration of his plan of grace, either Elohim or Jehovah would be in place, and it depends upon the writer's conception at the time which he will employ. It is not necessary, therefore, in Genesis any more than in other books of the Bible, to be able to show that there was a necessity for using that divine name which is actually employed. It is sufficient to show, as can invariably be done, that the writer might properly use the name which he has actually chosen. This fully refutes the purely mechanical view, which overlooks the difference in the meaning and usage of these names, and their appropriateness to the connection in which they are found, and sees in their alternation nothing but the unmeaning peculiarities of style of different writers.

II. The second argument in favor of the various partition hypotheses is drawn from the alleged fact that when the several sections or paragraphs, respectively assigned to the supposed writers separately, are put together they form a continuous and connected whole. But—

(1) The allegation is not well founded. It is only

they who have a theory to support who can fail to see
the chasms and abrupt transitions which are created by
the partition, and which require in order to fill them the
very passages which have been abstracted as belonging
to another document. Thus in ch. i. P gives an account
of the creation, and declares that God saw that everything
that he had made was very good. And then in vi. 11, 12,
without the slightest explanation, he suddenly announces
that the earth was corrupt before God and was filled with
violence so that he was determined to destroy it. This is
quite inexplicable without the account of the fall, which
has been sundered from it and given to J. In xix. 29
P tells what happened when God destroyed the cities of
the plain, without having before alluded to such a destruction as having occurred; the account of it is only to
be found in J. In xxviii. 1–5 P tells that Isaac sent
Jacob to Padan-aram to obtain a wife. But his entire
residence there, eventful as it was, is in P an absolute
blank. In xxxi. 18 he is said to be returning with goods
and cattle, and in xxxv. 22–26 his twelve children are enumerated, though no previous intimation had been given
by P of his having either property or a family. How all
this came about is related only in the other documents.
Numerous gaps and chasms of this nature are found in
each of the so-called documents, and are in every case
created by the critical partition. The critics undertake
to account for all such cases by saying that the redactor,
having given the narrative from one of his sources, designedly omits what is contained in the others to avoid
needless repetition. And yet in other cases we are told
that he scrupulously retains the contents of his different
sources, even though it leads to such superfluous repetitions as the double mention of Noah's entry into the ark
and of various particulars connected with the flood
as given both by J and P. They are besides perpetu-

ally drawing inferences that imply the completeness of the documents, as when they attribute to P the notion that sacrifice was first introduced by Moses; or when they interpret passages at variance with their context on the assumption that nothing had been joined with them like that from which the so-called critical analysis separates them. It is thus that the most of the alleged contrarieties are created. In fact critical partition would lose its chief interest and importance in the eyes of its advocates if they were not allowed in this manner to alter and even revolutionize the meaning of the sacred text.

(2) In many cases where continuity is claimed it is only accomplished by bridging evident gaps by means of scattered clauses sundered here and there from their proper connection, as is done for J in the account of the flood, and for P in the early history of Abraham. Or by alleging that the texts of two documents have been mixed, and because a paragraph attributed to one document contains occasional words or phrases which are assumed to be peculiar to another, inferring that these must have been taken from some imaginary parallel passage in that document, which is necessary to make out its continuity, as in both J and E in the history of Joseph.

(3) The apparent connection produced by bringing separated passages together and removing the intervening paragraphs or sections is altogether factitious. This may be so adroitly done that such passages will read continuously as though there had been no omission. But any other book can be subjected to the same mode of treatment with a like result. Paragraphs of greater or less extent can be removed from any piece of writing whatever without the reader suspecting it, unless he is informed of the fact.

(4) The proofs are abundant that each of the so-called

documents either directly alludes to, or presupposes, what is contained in the others. This is, of course, quite inconsistent with the hypothesis of their independent origin. The utmost pains have been taken by the critics to construct their documents so as to avoid this inter-relation ; but it has been impossible for them to prevent it altogether. Hence they are compelled to acknowledge their intimate connection. Kayser regards J as the redactor of JE ; Dillmann thinks that J possessed and often borrowed from E ; Jülicher that P drew from JE. Both the sameness of plan and the reciprocal relation of the narratives in all the so-called documents throughout the entire Pentateuchal history implies a dependence of one upon the other. This is admitted even by Wellhausen.

(5) The critics are in the habit of playing fast and loose with the criterion of continuity, which at times is their sole or chief dependence, and at others is disregarded entirely. While they profess to trace documents in a great measure by the connection of their several parts, they in numerous instances sunder what is most intimately bound together by necessary implications or express allusions, thus nullifying their own principal clew and invalidating their own conclusions.

III. The third argument in favor of the partition hypothesis is drawn from parallel passages, which are alleged to be separate accounts of the same thing taken from different documents. But—

(1) In many instances what are claimed as parallel sections are not really such, but relate to matters quite distinct, which, however, bear some resemblance to each other. Thus, to refer to an instance previously adduced, there is nothing surprising in the fact that Abraham should on two occasions have been betrayed into a prevarication respecting his wife. His having done so once in apprehended peril might easily incline him to do so

again in similar circumstances. And that Isaac, when similarly situated, should imitate the error of his father, is not at all incredible. All history would be thrown into confusion, if a mere general resemblance in different events were to lead to their identification. How easy it would be for some future historian to claim that the accounts of the different battles at Bull Run, in the late war of the rebellion, all issuing in one way, were merely varying traditions of one and the same. To infer the identity of the facts from the points of agreement in the narratives, and then the discrepancy in the statements regarding it from their disagreement in other points, which simply shows the facts to be distinct, is to construct a self-contradictory argument. Moreover, the assertion that what are recorded as distinct events are in reality variant accounts of one and the same thing, is made without the semblance of proof or evidence of any sort. It is simply based on the prior assumption of the untrustworthiness of the sacred historian. His explicit statement is set aside as valueless beside the arbitrary conjecture of the critic. This is not a conclusion established by the divisive criticism, but is assumed in advance as a basis on which the divisive criticism is itself built. This reveals the unfriendly animus of the current critical analysis, which is inwrought in it, and inseparable from it, and is one of the determining influences by which it has been shaped.

(2) Where the events referred to are the same, they are mentioned under a different aspect or adduced for a different purpose, which accounts for the repetition. Thus the renewed mention in Gen. ii. of the formation of man and the lower animals, which had already been spoken of in ch. i., is no proof that these are by separate writers ; for each chapter has a design of its own, which is steadfastly kept in view, the second being not parallel

to, but the sequel of, the first.   Noah's entry into the ark
is twice recorded, without, however, any implication that
two documents have here been drawn upon.   After the
general statement (vii. 7–9) that he went in with his family and various species of living things, the writer wishes
to emphasize more exactly that he went in on the very
same day that the flood began (vs. 13–16), and so restates
it with that view.

(3) In the simple style of Hebrew narrative it is usual
to make a summary statement at the outset, which is
then followed by a detailed account of the particulars included under it, and in recording the execution of a command to restate the injunctions to which obedience is
rendered.   The critics seize upon such passages and endeavor to turn them to the advantage of the partition
hypothesis, but in so doing sunder what evidently
belongs together.   Thus in Gen. xxviii. 5, it is said that
Isaac sent away Jacob and he went to Padan-aram, unto
Laban, the brother of Rebekah.   His actual journey is
described in xxviii. 10–xxix. 13.   The critics rend these
asunder, giving the former to P and the latter to JE.   In
like manner xxxi. 18 is a summary statement of Jacob's
leaving Padan-aram to go to Isaac, his father, unto the
land of Canaan.   This is followed by the details of his
journey (xxxi. 20–xxxiii. 17), all which is given to JE,
while the preliminary statement is assigned to P.   So
the account of Jacob's funeral (l. 4–11) is given to J,
the summary statement of the burial (vs. 12, 13) to P.
A like severance of what is closely related is made where
directions are given and carried into effect.   Thus Sarah
proposes to Abraham that he should take Hagar as his
wife, to which he consents (xvi. 2) ; this is given to J.
But the carrying of this proposal into effect (ver. 3) is
given to P.   The LORD bids Moses tell the children of
Israel how to observe the passover (Ex. xii. 2–20) ; this is

given to P. In obedience to this direction Moses summons the elders and explains the observance to them (vs. 21-27); this is given to J.

(4) Wellhausen and Dillmann have pushed the partition by means of alleged parallels to the most extravagant lengths by what they call doublets. This brings the subdivision down in many cases to minute paragraphs, or even single clauses. In a transaction which is accomplished by successive steps or stages, any one of these steps may be regarded as the doublet of another at the pleasure of the critic; that is to say, they may be considered as variant statements of the same thing by a different writer and accordingly assigned to distinct documents. Or any repetition of the same thought in varied language, by which the writer would emphasize his statement or more fully explain his meaning, may be reckoned a doublet, and the clauses partitioned accordingly. Thus in Gen. xxxvii. two things are recited which awakened the hatred of Joseph's brethren; first (vs. 3, 4), his father's partiality for him, secondly (vs. 5-11), his dreams, which he related to them. These statements supplement each other, and must be combined in order to a complete view of the grounds of their hostility. But they are converted into two different modes of accounting for the same thing, the former being the conception entertained by J, the latter that of E. Again, a doublet is found in the two clauses of xxi. 1, " The LORD visited Sarah as he had said, and the LORD did unto Sarah as he had spoken." These are reckoned equivalents, and are divided between J and P, whereas the second is additional to, and explanatory of, the meaning of the first.

The alleged doublets, incoherences, and inconsistencies, by which the attempt is made to bolster up the weakness of other arguments for the original separateness of J and E, are capable of being set aside in detail. They are for the most part hypercritical cavilling, magnifying molehills into mountains, and measuring ancient oriental narratives by the rules of modern occidental discourse.

IV. The fourth argument is based upon alleged differences of diction, style, and ideas. The process by which these are ascertained is that of instituting at the beginning a careful comparison of two sections, supposed to be from different documents, such as the first two sections of Genesis. All differences of thought and language between them are minutely noted, and the comparison is then extended to contiguous sections, and so on, gradually and guardedly, to the remaining portions of the Pentateuch, all being assigned to one or the other document on the basis of the criteria already gathered, and which are constantly accumulating as the work proceeds ; the utmost pains being taken so to adjust the sections that all references from one to the other shall fall within the limits of the same document, and that the intervening passages which are given to the other document shall not be missed. But notwithstanding the seeming plausibility of this method, and the apparent scientific caution and accuracy with which it is conducted, it is altogether fallacious. For—

(1) The argument is simply reasoning in a circle. The differences are first created and then argued from. The documents are first framed to correspond with certain assumed characteristic differences, and then their correspondence with these characteristics is urged in proof of their objective reality. All paragraphs, clauses, and parts of clauses, in which a certain class of alleged criteria occur, are systematically assigned to one document, and those having another class of criteria are, with like regularity, assigned to another document ; and

8

when the process is complete, all the criteria of one class are in one document, and those of the other class are in the other document, simply because the critic has put them there. The documents accord with the hypothesis because they have been constructed by the hypothesis.

(2) The proofs relied upon for diversity of diction are factitious, and can be applied with like effect to any book of any author. All words in one of the so-called documents which do not chance to be found in the others are carefully gathered out and strung together in a formidable list. Any one treatise of an author can in this way equally be made to prove that any other of his treatises was not written by him, or any part of one to prove that the remaining portion came from another hand. That certain words which occur in one series of paragraphs or sections do not occur in another proves nothing unless it can be shown that the writer had occasion to use them. Especially is this the case when the words adduced are in familiar and common use, or are the only words suited to express a given idea; these obviously cannot be classed as the peculium of any one writer.[1] Also when they are of infrequent occurrence, and so give no indication of a writer's habitual usage, or are words belonging to one particular species of composition. It is not surprising that poetic words should not be found in a document from which poetic passages are systematically excluded; or that legal words and phrases should be limited to the document to which the legal passages are regularly assigned; or that words appropriate to ordinary narrative should

[1] My friend Professor McCurdy, of Toronto University, pertinently suggests in a private note that much of the critical argument from diction would prove too much if it proved anything. If words of this description furnish a criterion, it would imply not merely a diversity of writers, but writers using different dialects or languages.

chiefly abound in those documents to which the bulk of such narrative is given. Since the entire ritual law is given to P, and the great body of the history, together with all the poetical passages, to JE, a corresponding difference of diction and style must necessarily result from this diversity of theme, and of the character of the composition, without being by any means suggestive of a difference of writers. When the words alleged to be characteristic of one of the documents occur but rarely in that document, and are absent from the great majority of its sections, this must, on the critical hypothesis, be regarded as accidental; so may their absence from the sections of the other document be.

It must also be remembered that a writer who has a reasonable command of language may vary his expressions in conveying the same idea. It is not a safe assumption that he cannot use words or phrases in any place which he has not used elsewhere. Thus Dillmann (" Die Bücher, Exodus und Leviticus," p. 619), argues that a peculiar diction is not always indicative of separate authorship. After saying that the passage of which he is speaking has some of the characteristics of J, but " much more that is unusual and peculiar," he adds, " The most of this nature may be accounted for partly by the poetic and oratorical style, and partly by the new and peculiar objects and ideas that were to be expressed, and it can scarcely suffice to justify the conclusion of an altogether peculiar writer, from whom we have nothing besides."

(3) When synonymous expressions are used to convey the same idea this does not justify the assumption that they have been taken from different documents, and that they severally represent the usage of distinct writers. They are not to be explained in this superficial and mechanical manner. Synonyms are not usually exact

counterparts. There is commonly a distinction, more or less clear, which may be observed between them, some slight difference in their meaning or their association, which governs their employment and leads to the use of one rather than another in particular connections.

(4) The alleged criteria frequently conflict with each other, and with the criteria derived from the divine names. Words or phrases said to be characteristic of one writer meet in the same section, or even in the same sentence, with those that are said to characterize the other. In such cases the critics resort to various subterfuges to relieve the situation. Sometimes they admit that what has been considered characteristic of one document is found likewise in another, which is equivalent to a confession that it is not a distinctive criterion at all. At other times they claim that two texts have been mingled, and that expressions or clauses from one document have been interpolated in the other, whereas these blended criteria simply prove that the same writer freely uses both in the same connection. Again, at other times they claim that such passages belong originally to neither document, but are insertions by the redactor, who is always at hand to account for phenomena at variance with the hypothesis, when no other mode of escape is possible. It is obviously possible by such devices to carry through any hypothesis, however preposterous. If all opposing phenomena can be set aside as interpolations, or as the work of the redactor, the most refractory texts can be tortured into accordance with the critic's arbitrary presuppositions.

(5) The critic is engaged in solving an indeterminate equation. The line of partition depends upon the criteria, and the criteria depend upon the line of partition; and both of these are unknown quantities. Of necessity the work is purely hypothetical from first to

last, and the liability to error increases with every step of the process. A mistake in the criteria will lead to a wrong partition, and this to further false criteria, and so on indefinitely ; and there is no sure method of correcting or even ascertaining the error. The critic resembles a traveller who without guide or compass is seeking to make his way through a trackless forest, so dense as to shut out the sight of the heavens. He will inevitably diverge from a straight course, and may gradually and imperceptibly be turned in the opposite direction from that in which he started. Or he may prove to be only a dreamer, whose beautiful creations are but airy phantoms.

(6) The complexity of the problem with which the critic has undertaken to deal becomes more obvious the further he proceeds. At the outset his work is comparatively simple; the fewer the criteria the more readily they are applied. By the aid of such ingenious devices as have already been indicated he makes his way through Genesis with tolerable ease. But in the middle books of the Pentateuch difficulties crowd upon him, as is shown by the wide divergence of the critics in their efforts to cope with them, and in the book of Joshua it becomes a veritable medley. It is the natural result of an attempt to apply criteria gathered elsewhere to fresh passages for which they have no affinity. Partitions are made which find no sanction in an unbiassed examination of the passages themselves, and are merely forced upon them for the sake of consistency with a previously adopted scheme of division. This is repeatedly confessed by the critics themselves. Thus Wellhausen,[1] in beginning his discussion of Gen. xxxvii.–l. says: " The principal source for this last section of Genesis also is

---

[1] Jahrbücher für Deutsche Theologie, 1876, p. 442, or in the separate reprint, Die Composition des Hexateuchs, p. 52.

JE. It is to be presumed that this work, here as elsewhere, is compounded of J and E; our former results constrain to this assumption, and would be shaken if this were not capable of proof."

The various arguments urged in support of the divisive hypothesis in its different forms have now been successively examined and found wanting. The alternation of divine names can be otherwise explained, and moreover it can only be brought into harmony with the partition hypothesis by a free use of the redactor, and the assumption of repeated changes of the text. Ex. vi. 3 has not the meaning that the critics attribute to it. The continuity of the documents is broken by serious chasms, or maintained by very questionable methods; and it is necessary to assume in numerous instances that the documents originally contained paragraphs and sections similar to those which the critics have sundered from them. The alleged parallel passages are for the most part falsely assumed identifications of distinct events. And the diversity of diction, style, and ideas is made out by utterly fallacious and inconclusive methods. But while the attempted proof of lack of unity signally fails, the positive evidence of unity abides and never can be nullified. The great outstanding proof of it is the unbroken continuity of the history, the consistent plan upon which the whole is prepared, and the numerous cross-references, which bind it all together as the work of one mind. Separate and independent documents mechanically pieced together could no more produce such an appearance of unity as reigns throughout the Pentateuch than a faultless statue could be formed out of discordant fragments of dissimilar materials.

The futility of the methods by which the Pentateuch has been parcelled into different documents may further be shown by the readiness with which they can be applied, and with equal success, to writings the unity of which is indisputable.   The fact that a narrative can be so divided as to form from it two continuous narratives, is reckoned by the critics a demonstration of its composite character, and a proof that the parts into which it has been severed are the original sources from which it has been compounded.   This may be tested by a couple of passages selected at random—the parables of **The Prodigal Son** and of **The Good Samaritan.**

THE PRODIGAL SON, Luke xv. 11–32.

A

B

11. A certain man had two sons : 12. and the younger of them said to his father, Father, give me the portion of thy substance that falleth to me.   .   .   . 13. And not many days after the younger son gathered all together,   .   .   . and there he wasted his substance with riotous living.   .   .   .

(A certain man had **two sons :**)

14b. **and he began to be in want.**

12b. and he **divided unto** them his living.

13b. And (one of them) took his journey into a far country.   .   .   . 14. And when he had spent all, there arose a mighty famine in that country.   .   .   . 15. And he went and joined himself to one of the citizens of that country ; and he sent him into his fields to feed swine.   16. And he would fain have been filled with the husks that the swine did eat.   .   .   . 17. But when he came to himself he said, How many hired servants of my father's have bread enough and to spare, and I perish here with hunger !   18. I will arise and go to my father, and will **say unto**

16b. **And no man gave unto** him. 20. And he arose, and came to his father ;   .   .   . and he ran, and fell on his neck, and kissed him.   21. And the son said unto him, Father, I have sinned

A

against heaven, and in thy sight : I am no more worthy to be called thy son. 22. But the father said to his servants, Bring forth quickly the best robe, and put it on him ; and put a ring on his hand, and shoes on his feet: . . . 24. for this my son was dead, and is alive again. . . . And they began to be merry. 25. Now his elder son was in the field : and as he came and drew nigh to the house, . . . 28. he was angry, and would not go in : and his father came out, and entreated him. 29. But he answered and said to his father, Lo, these many years do I serve thee, and I never transgressed a commandment of thine : and yet thou never gavest me a kid, that I might make merry with my friends : 30. but when this thy son came, which hath devoured thy living with harlots, thou killedst for him the fatted calf. 31. And he said unto him, Son, thou art ever with me, and all that is mine is thine. 32. But it was meet to make merry and be glad : for this thy brother was dead, and is alive again.

B

him, Father, I have sinned against heaven, and in thy sight : 19. I am no more worthy to be called thy son : make me as one of thy hired servants. . . . 20b. But while he was yet afar off, his father saw him, and was moved with compassion : . . . 23. and (said) Bring the fatted calf, and kill it, and let us eat, and make merry. . . . 24b. he was lost, and is found. . . . 25b. (And the other son) heard music and dancing. 26. And he called to him one of the servants, and inquired what these things might be. 27. And he said unto him, Thy brother is come ; and thy father hath killed the fatted calf, because he hath received him safe and sound . . . 32b. and he was lost and is found.

There are here two complete narratives, agreeing in some points, and disagreeing in others, and each has its special characteristics. The only deficiencies are enclosed in parentheses, and may be readily explained as omissions by the redactor in effecting the combination. A clause must be supplied at the beginning of B, a subject is wanting in ver. 13b, and ver. 25b, and the verb "said" is wanting in ver. 23. As these omissions occur exclusively in B, it may be inferred that the redactor placed A at the basis, and incorporated B into it with only such slight changes as were necessary to adapt it to this purpose.

A and B agree that there were two sons, one of whom received a portion of his father's property, and by his own fault was reduced to great destitution, in consequence of which he returned penitently to his father, and addressed him in language which is nearly identical in both accounts. The father received him with great tenderness and demonstrations of joy, which attracted the attention of the other son.

The differences are quite as striking as the points of agreement. A distinguishes the sons as elder and younger; B makes no mention of their relative ages. In A the younger obtained his portion by solicitation, and the father retained the remainder in his own possession; in B the father divided his property between both of his sons of his own motion. In A the prodigal remained in his father's neighborhood, and reduced himself to penury by riotous living; in B he went to a distant country and spent all his property, but there is no intimation that he indulged in unseemly excesses. It would rather appear that he was injudicious; and to crown his misfortunes there occurred a severe famine. His fault seems to have consisted in having gone so far away from his father and from the holy land, and in engaging in the unclean occupation of tending swine. In A the destitution seems to have been chiefly want of clothing; in B want of food. Hence in A the father directed the best robe and ring and shoes to be brought for him; in B the fatted calf was killed. In B the son came from a distant land, and the father saw him afar off; in A he came from the neighborhood, and the father ran at once and fell on his neck and kissed him. In B he had been engaged in a menial occupation, and so bethought himself of his father's hired servants, and asked to be made a servant himself; in A he had been living luxuriously, and while confessing his unworthiness makes no request to be put on the footing of a servant. In A the father speaks of his son having been dead because of his profligate life; in B of his having been lost because of his absence in a distant land. In A, but not in B, the other son was displeased at the reception given to the prodigal. And here it would appear that R has slightly altered the text. The elder son must have said to his father in A, "When this thy son came, which hath devoured thy substance with harlots, thou didst put on him the best robe." The redactor has here substituted the B word "living" [1] for "substance," which is used by A; and with the view of making a better contrast with "kid" he has introduced the B phrase, "thou killedst for him the fatted calf."

THE GOOD SAMARITAN, Luke x. 29–37.

A	B
29. But he (the lawyer, ver. 25) desiring to justify himself, said unto Jesus, And who is my neighbor? 30. Jesus made answer and said, A certain man was going down from Jerusalem to Jericho; . . . and they beat him, . . . leaving him half dead. 31. And by chance a certain priest was going down that	30b. And (a certain man) * fell among robbers, which both stripped him . . . and departed. . . . * Omitted by R. ( ).

[1] No scholar will need to be informed that "living" ver. 13, has a different sense and represents a different word in the original from "living," ver. 12.

A

way : and when he saw him, he passed by on the other side. . . . 33. But a certain Samaritan, as he journeyed, came where he was : . . . 34. and came to him, and bound up his wounds, pouring on them oil and wine, . . . and took care of him.

36 Which of these [three]*, thinkest thou, proved neighbor unto him ? . . . 37. And he said, He that showed mercy on him.

B

32. And [in like manner] * a Levite, [also] * when he came to the place, [and saw him, passed by on the other side.] * 33b. and when he saw him, was moved with compassion. . . . 34b. And he set him on his own beast, and brought him to an inn. . . . 35. And on the morrow he took out two pence, and gave them to the host, and said, Take care of him ; and whatsoever thou spendest more, I, when I come back again, will repay thee. 37b. And Jesus said unto him . . . that fell among the robbers, . . . Go, and do thou likewise.

* Inserted by R [   ].

Both these narratives are complete ; only a subject must be supplied in B, ver. 30b, the omission of which was rendered necessary by its being combined with A. "Three" is substituted for "two" in A, ver. 36, for a like reason. R has tampered with the text and materially altered the sense in ver. 32, from his desire to put the Levite on the same plane with the priest in ver. 31, the language of which he has borrowed ; the genuine text of B will be restored by omitting the insertions by R, which are included in brackets. He has likewise transposed a brief clause of B, in ver. 37b, and added it at the end of ver. 36. These changes naturally resulted from his making A the basis, and modifying what he has inserted from B into accordance with it. Hence the necessity of making it appear that it was not the Levite, but the Samaritan, who befriended the injured traveller, and that

Jesus spoke not to the traveller, but to the lawyer. In all other respects the original texts of the two narratives remain unaltered.

Both narratives agree that a man grievously abused by certain parties was treated with generous kindness by a stranger; and that Jesus deduced a practical lesson from it. But they differ materially in details.

A relates his story as a parable of Jesus in answer to a lawyer's question. B makes no mention of the lawyer or his question, but seems to be relating a real occurrence.

The spirit of the two is quite different. A is anti-Jewish, B pro-Jewish. In A the aggressors are Jews, people of Jerusalem or Jericho or both, and a priest pitilessly leaves the sufferer to his fate; while it is a Samaritan, with whom the Jews were in perpetual feud, who takes pity on him. In B the aggressors are robbers, outlaws whose nationality is not defined, and it is a Levite who shows mercy.

Both the maltreatment and the act of generosity are different. In A the sufferer is beaten and half killed, and needs to have his wounds bound up and liniments applied, which is done by his benefactor on the spot. In B he was stripped of all he had and left destitute, but no personal injury was inflicted; accordingly he was taken to an inn, and his wants there provided for at the expense of the Levite who befriended him.

The lesson inculcated is different. In A it is that the duty of loving one's neighbor is not limited to those of the same nation, nor annulled by national antipathies. In B it is that he who has been befriended himself should befriend others.

It is not worth while to multiply illustrations. Those now adduced are sufficient to give an idea of the method by which the critics undertake to effect the partition of the Pentateuch ; and to show how they succeed in creating discrepancies and contradictions, where none really exist, by simply sundering what properly belongs together. The ease with which these results can be accomplished, where obviously they have no possible significance, shows how fallacious and inconclusive this style of argument is. No dependence can be placed upon a process that leads to palpably erroneous conclusions in other cases. An argument that will prove everything, proves nothing. And a style of critical analysis which can be made to prove everything composite is not to be trusted.

The readiness with which a brief, simple narrative yields to critical methods has been sufficiently shown above. That extended didactic composition is not proof against it is shown in a very clever and effective manner in " Romans Dissected," by E. D. McRealsham, the pseudonym of Professor C. M. Mead, D.D., of Hartford Theological Seminary. The result of his ingenious and scholarly discussion is to demonstrate that as plausible an argument can be made from diction, style, and doctrinal contents for the fourfold division of the Epistle to the Romans as for the composite character of the Pentateuch.

Two additional incongruities which beset the partition of the Pentateuch may be briefly mentioned here, as they are illustrated by the specimens above given of the application of like methods to the parables. The first is, that the narratives into which the critics resolve the Pentateuchal history, and from which they claim that this has been compounded, are, as a whole and in all their parts, inferior in symmetry and structural arrangement to the history as it lies in the existing text. On the critical hypothesis precisely the reverse should be the case. If the history is a conglomerate, in which hetero-

geneous materials have been compacted, the critical sev‑
erance which restores the component parts to their orig‑
inal connection and exhibits each of the primary narra‑
tives in its pristine form, and purged of all interpolations
and extraneous matter, must remove disfigurements and
reunite the broken links of connection designed by the
early narrators. The intermingling of goods of different
patterns has a confusing effect. It is only when they are
separated, and each is viewed by itself, that its proper
pattern can be traced and its real beauty discerned.
But when the separation spoils and mars the fabric, we
must conclude that what has taken place is not the reso‑
lution of a compound into its primary constituents, but
the violent rending asunder of what was really a unit,
the breaking of a graceful statue into misshapen frag‑
ments.

The second incongruity to be alluded to here concerns
what the critics consider the restored original narratives,
not taken separately, each by itself, but in their relation
to one another. The critics take what in its present
form, as it lies before us in the Pentateuch, is harmoni‑
ous, symmetrical, and complete, and they deduce from it
two or more narratives, between which there are discrep‑
ancies, contrarieties, and contradictions; and these are
produced simply by the putting asunder of what in the
existing text to all appearance properly belongs together.
And it thereby writes its own condemnation. Harmony
does not arise from combining the incongruous, but dis‑
cord naturally follows upon the derangement of parts,
which properly fitted into one another are harmonious.

A word may further be added concerning the marvellous
perspicacity, verging on omniscience, claimed by the crit‑
ics, who undertake to determine with the utmost assurance
the authorship not merely of books, or large sections or
paragraphs, but of individual sentences and clauses, and

fragments of clauses. They undertake to point out to
the very last degree of nicety and minuteness not only
what J and E and D and P have separately written, however involved these may be with one another, but what
precise changes each of a series of redactors has introduced into the original text of each, and what glosses
have been added by a still later hand, and what modifications were introduced into the successive editions
through which the principal documents have severally
passed before or since their combination. They further
profess to be able to distinguish the primary and sometimes discordant elements which entered into the original constitution of the principal documents, and what
belongs to the various stages by which P was brought
by a series of diaskeuasts to its present complexity and
elaboration. One would think that the critics would be
awed by the formidable character of the task which they
have set for themselves. But they proceed with un-
daunted front, as though they had an unerring scent
which could track their game through the most intricate
doublings and convolutions; and as though positive as-
sertions would compensate for the dubious nature of the
grounds upon which their decisions often rest.

If further proof were needed of the precarious character
of the methods and results of this style of subjective
criticism, it is abundantly supplied by similar exploits
conducted in other fields, where they can be subjected to
the sure test of ascertained facts. The havoc wrought in
the writings of Homer, belonging to a remote antiquity,
or in the "Nibelungenlied," produced in the obscurity of
the Middle Ages, is not so much to our present purpose
as the systematic onset upon Cicero's orations against
Catiline, of whose genuineness there is indubitable proof.
Madvig's account of the matter, to which my attention
was directed by Professor West, of Princeton University,

and of which he has obligingly furnished the translation, is here given in a note.[1]

[1] " Let us relate the history of the discussion. It began with F. A. Wolf,* who cast doubt in a general way upon several of Cicero's Orations. Following Wolf came Eichstaedt, who reviewed Wolf's book in 1802, and took the position that at least one of the Catilinarian Orations ought to be included in the condemnation bestowed upon other orations. Wolf quickly followed Eichstaedt and condemned the Third Oration, and in subsequent comments and remarks stated the question in such a way as to leave it uncertain which oration he meant, or whether it was one of two orations, and so, in 1826, Clude, thinking he was following out the opinion of Wolf, proved to his own satisfaction and the satisfaction of some others, that it was the Second Oration which was spurious. But shortly afterward (in 1827) Benecke, by producing the very words of Wolf from one of his letters showed that Wolf meant the Third Oration. In the meantime the Fourth Oration had fallen under the displeasure of other critics, notably Zimmermann and Bloch, and so Ahrens, in 1832, passed sentence on the unfortunate oration, embracing the Third Oration at the same time in his condemnation. Finally came Orelli, in 1836, and fearing, I suppose, that such inconsistencies of opinion would end in contempt and ridicule, decided that all three were spurious.

" In addition to other evidence from ancient writers which was easily answered, there stood opposed to this conclusion the authority of Cicero himself, who in the First Epistle of the Second Book of his Letters to Atticus makes abundant reference to his own consular orations, and *enumerates one by one the four Orations against Catiline.*

" And so no other course was left the critics except to come to the incredible conclusion that genuine orations of Cicero, delivered on a most famous occasion, had so faded out of remembrance by the time of Augustus (for Ahrens admits that the orations we possess are as old as this) that spurious orations could be put in their place and meet with acceptance, without any contemporary objection, in spite of the fact that one genuine oration out of the four still remained, and was put together with the three false ones. Orelli met the emergency heroically (*forti remedio*), for he cut out the whole of this passage from the middle of Cicero's Letter to Atticus. Consequently no statement remained regarding the various Catilinarian orations published by Cicero himself. Thereupon Orelli excogitated a pleasant hypothesis (*fabulam lepidam*) to the effect that a forger first supplied the three orations, and then, in order to insure their acceptance, inserted in the Letter of Cicero a forged

* The critic of Homer and father of the destructive literary criticism.

My colleague, Dr. Warfield, has also pointed me to an instructive instance which is still more recent. It is thus described by Dr. Heinrici:[1] "How easily one is led astray by assuming a course of thought supposed to be requisite, is shown in a very instructive man-

statement in regard to these same orations. But inasmuch as Cicero's Letters were then in circulation, we might ask, How was it that this forger inserted his forgery not only in his own copy of Cicero's Letters, but in the copies of all other readers whom he wished to deceive, and so managed it that no other copy of this Letter should remain extant written in any other manner? But the same critical shrewdness helps the critics at this juncture. The forger is that very man who edited the volume of Letters after Cicero's death, namely, Marcus Tullius Tiro, the freedman. What! Tiro, the faithful freedman to whom Cicero entrusted his Letters, and who wrote the life of his dead patron accurately and affectionately, and upon whom no suspicion ever fell, was he a forger? 'Yes, indeed,' they answered, 'and he did it with good intention.' Orelli says, 'He thought that he would honor his noble patron most if Cicero's illustrious performance were made celebrated not merely by one but by four orations.' What a marvellous license of imagination and credulity of doubt! So, then, Tiro did not think the matter would be famous by reason of his narrative of Cicero's life, but, although he had never uttered a word in a public assembly, or written even a short oration, he yet thought that the glory of his patron, the greatest orator of Rome, would be increased by Tiro's forging orations under Cicero's name. Yet why not? For the very critic, who is everywhere finding fault with the wretched inconsistencies of Tiro's writings, yet in former times had actually admired Cicero on account of these false orations."—Madvig: Opuscula Academica, Hauniae, 1887, pp. 671 sqq.

Dr. West adds: "Madvig's *reductio ad absurdum* is complete. There are numerous other instances in Latin criticism that are instructive. Ribbeck's youthful venture at the text of Juvenal, Peerlkamp's exploits in Horace, the discussion forty years ago regarding the treatise *De Trinitate*, ascribed to Boethius, and the treatment of Cæsar's Commentaries on the Gallic War, ought not to be forgotten. Schoell's slashing editing of Plautus in our own time is also a case in point. Happily the spirit which at present rules Latin studies is historical and inductive. The other reminds us of the old proverb about the Sabines —*Sabini quod volunt somniant.*"

[1] Meyer's Kommentar über den 1 Cor., seventh edit., 1888, Vorrede.

9

ner by Scherer's ingenious analysis of the Prologue
of Faust in his Goethe-Studies. It should set up a
beacon to warn classical philologists against overhasty
interpolation-criticism, since it shows how in a piece of
writing, whose composition by one author is beyond
question, profound diversities of style and inner contradictions exist. Scherer proposes to explain them from
differences in the time of composition and subsequent
combination. And now the oldest manuscript of Faust
has been published by Erich Schmidt, which proves that
it was the 'young Goethe' who wrote the prologue at
one effort essentially as it now stands. It is the same
'young Goethe' who speaks both in the ferment of
youth and in a disillusioned old age."

It has been claimed that the general agreement among
critics of various schools in regard to the partition is such
as to establish in the main the correctness of their conclusions. Where not only avowed antisupernaturalists
like Wellhausen, Kuenen, and Stade, but Dillmann, who
openly antagonizes them, and believing scholars like
Delitzsch and Driver are in accord, are we not con-
strained to yield assent to their positions? To this we
reply:

1. That this is not a question to be decided by authority but by reason and argument.

2. The consensus of divisive critics settles, not the
truth of the hypothesis, but what they consider its most
plausible and defensible form. The partition of the
Pentateuch is a definite problem with certain data, to
which any solution that is offered must adapt itself.
Experiments without number have been made to ascertain the practicability of this partition, and what lines of
division offer the best chance of success. The ground
has been surveyed inch by inch with the most scrupulous
care, its possibilities ascertained, and diligent search

made for the best methods of guarding weak points,
protecting against assault, overcoming difficulties, closing up gaps, and dealing with intractable passages.
And the present agreement of critics, so far as it goes,
indicates what is believed to be the most practicable
mode of carrying out the hypothesis that has yet been
devised.

3. The agreement of the critics is by no means perfect. While at many points there is a general consent,
at others there is wide divergence. Dillmann differs
from Wellhausen, and he from Kuenen, and Jülicher
from them all. Many are content to follow the prominent leaders more or less implicitly, but critics of independence and originality continue to propose new expe-
dients and offer fresh conjectures. Difficulties gather as
the work proceeds. In large portions of Genesis there is
comparative agreement ; in the middle books of the Pentateuch the diversities greatly multiply ; and in Joshua,
the crown of the Hexateuch, there is the most discordant
medley.

4. A large number of eminent scholars accept the
critical partition of the Pentateuch in general, if not in
all its details. It has its fascinations, which sufficiently
account for its popularity. The learning, ability, and
patient toil which have been expended upon its elaboration, the specious arguments arrayed in its support, and
the skill with which it has been adapted to the phenomena of the Pentateuch and of the Old Testament generally, have given to it the appearance of great plausibility.
The novel lines of inquiry which it opens make it attrac-
tive to those of a speculative turn of mind, who see in
it the opportunity for original and fruitful research in
the reproduction of ancient documents, long buried unsuspected in the existing text, which they antedate by
centuries. The boldness and seeming success with

which it undertakes to revolutionize traditional opinion, and give a new aspect to the origin and history of the religion of the Old Testament, and its alliance with the doctrine of development, which has found such wide application in other fields of investigation, have largely contributed to its popularity. And those who have a bias against the supernatural or the divine authority of the Pentateuch see in this hypothesis a ready way of disposing of its Mosaic origin and of the historic truth of whatever they are indisposed to accept.

The various forms of the partition hypothesis and the several arguments by which they are supported have now been examined. The arguments have been found inadequate and it will elsewhere be shown in detail that the hypothesis cannot be fitted to the phenomena of the Pentateuch.[1] Its failure is not from the lack of ingenuity or learning, or persevering effort on the part of its advocates, nor from the want of using the utmost latitude of conjecture, but simply from the impossibility of accomplishing the end proposed. While, however, the hypothesis has proved futile as an attempt to account for the origin of the Pentateuch, the labor spent upon it has not been entirely thrown away, and it has not been without positive advantage to the cause of truth. (1) It has demonstrated the impossibility of such a partition. The experiment has been tried in every way that the utmost ingenuity could devise, but without success. (2) It has led to the development of a vast mass of positive evidence of unity, which would not otherwise have been so diligently sought for, and might not have been

[1] Its incompatibility with the book of Genesis is demonstrated in a companion volume, The Unity of the Book of Genesis. The reader is likewise referred to the discussion of the remaining books of the Pentateuch in articles by the author in the Hebraica for 1890 and subsequently.

brought to light. (3) It has led to the elucidation and better understanding of the Pentateuch from the necessity thus imposed of minute and thorough investigation of the meaning and bearings of every word and sentence, and of the mutual relations of every part. It verifies the old fable of a field which was dug over for a chimerical purpose, but the labor thus expended was rewarded by an unlooked-for harvest, sprung from seed which lay unsuspected in the soil.[1]

[1] Crisis Hupfeldiana, by W. Kay, D.D., Oxford and London, 1865, is a trenchant review of Hupfeld's hypothesis as set forth in Bishop Colenso's Pentateuch and Joshua, Part V.

The Elements of the Higher Criticism, by Professor A. C. Zenos, New York, London, and Toronto, 1895, is a very clear and satisfactory presentation of the nature and objects of the higher criticism, together with its methods and its history, both in its application to the Old and to the New Testament.

V

GENUINENESS OF THE LAWS

THE first and second stages of opposition to the Mosaic authorship of the Pentateuch have now been reviewed. There yet remain to be considered the third and fourth lines of objection, which are based upon the triplicity of the legal codes and the non-observance of the laws. This brings us to the third and last stage of opposition.

The next phase of the critical movement, which issued in the present reigning school of divisive criticism, wrought as sudden and complete a revolution in the ideas of scholars of this class as the speculations of Darwin effected in Natural History, when the denial of the unity of the human race collapsed on the instant, and it was held instead that all animated being had sprung from common germs. And the lever which effected the overthrow was in both cases the same, that is, the doctrine of development. This at once exalted the speculations of Ewald and Hupfeld to a prominence which they had not previously attained, and made them important factors in the new advance. From Ewald was borrowed the idea that the composition of the Pentateuch was not accomplished at a stroke by one act, whether of supplementing or of combining pre-existing documents, but took place in successive stages by a series of enlarging combinations. From Hupfeld were derived the two pillars of his scheme—the continuity of the Jehovist document and the composite character of the Elohist—or, in other words, that the Jehovist did not merely make additions to a pre-existing work, but wrote an independent work of his own, and that there were two Elohists instead of one. Thus both Ewald and Hupfeld, without intending or imagining it, smoothed the way for the rise of a school of criticism with ideas quite diverse from their own.

The various attempts to partition the Pentateuch had thus far been based on exclusively literary grounds. Diction, style, ideas, the connection of paragraphs and sentences supplied the staple arguments for each of the forms which the hypothesis had assumed, and furnished the criteria from which all conclusions were drawn. Numerous efforts had been made to ascertain the dates to which the writers severally belonged. Careful studies were instituted to discover the bias under which they respectively wrote, as suggesting the influences by which they might be supposed to be surrounded, and hence their historical situation. They were diligently searched for historical allusions that might afford clews. But with all the pains that were taken no sure footing could be found, and the critics agreed not together. Conjectures ranged *ad libitum* through the ages from the time of Moses, or his immediate successor, Joshua, to that of Josiah, eight centuries later. And while the internal criteria were so vague, there was no external support on which the whole hypothesis could rest, no objective proof that the entire fabric was not a sheer figment of the imagination. Amid all diversities, however, two points were universally agreed upon, and regarded as settled beyond contradiction : (1) The Elohist was the groundwork of the Pentateuch ; it supplied the scheme or general plan, into which the other parts were fitted. And as it was the oldest, so it was historically the most reliable and trustworthy portion. The Jehovist was more legendary, depending, as it was believed to do, upon later and less credible traditions. (2) Deuteronomy was the latest and the crowning portion of the Pentateuch, by the addition of which the whole work was rendered complete.

DEVELOPMENT HYPOTHESIS.

Here the Development Hypothesis came in with its revolutionary conclusions. It supplied the felt lack of its predecessors by fixing definite dates and offering objective proof of their correctness. The conclusions deduced from the examination of the Pentateuch itself are verified by an appeal to the history. Arguments are drawn, not as heretofore, from the narratives of the Pentateuch but from its institutions; not from its historical portion but from its laws. The principle of development is applied. The simplest forms of legislation are to be considered the most primitive. As the Israelites developed in the course of ages from rude nomadic tribes to a settled and well-organized nation, their legislation naturally grew in complexity and extent. Now the Pentateuch obviously contains three distinct codes or bodies of law. One is in Exodus xx.–xxiii. which is called in the original text the Book of the Covenant (Ex. xxiv. 7). This Moses is said to have written and read to the assembled people at Mount Sinai as the basis of the covenant relation there formally ratified between Jehovah and Israel. Another is the Deuteronomic Law, which Moses is said to have rehearsed to the people in the plains of Moab, shortly before his death, and to have delivered in writing to the custody of the priests, to be laid up alongside of the ark of the covenant (Deut. xxxi. 24–26). A third is the Ritual law, or Priest code, contained in the later chapters of Exodus, the book of Leviticus, and certain chapters of

Numbers. This law is declared in the general and in all its parts to have been communicated by God to Moses.

The advocates of this hypothesis, however, take issue with these explicit statements, and affirm that these codes could not have had the origin attributed to them. It is maintained that they are so diverse in character and so inconsistent in their provisions that they cannot have originated at any one time or have proceeded from any one legislator. The Book of the Covenant, from its simplicity and brevity, must have belonged to an early stage in the history of the people. From this there is a great advance in the Deuteronomic code. And the Ritual law, or Priest code, is much the most minute and complicated of all, and hence the latest in the series. Long periods must have elapsed, and great changes have taken place in the condition of the people to have wrought such changes in their institutions.

The Book of the Covenant makes no mention of a priesthood, as a separate order of men alone authorized to perform sacred functions. The Deuteronomic code speaks of priests, who are constantly designated " the priests, the Levites," from which it is inferred that the sacerdotal prerogative inhered in the tribe as such, and that any Levite might be a priest. The Priest code limits the sacerdotal office to the family of Aaron : other Levites were simply their servants and attendants, performing menial functions at the sanctuary, but not allowed to offer sacrifice.

In the Book of the Covenant sacrifices are not regulated by statute, but are the free, spontaneous gift of the offerer unto God, in grateful acknowledgment of the divine benefits. In Deuteronomy certain kinds of offerings are specified, but with no fixed requisition of number and quality, and these are to be joyously partaken of by the offerer and his family and friends before the LORD.

In the Levitical code additional kinds of sacrifice are required, not mentioned elsewhere, and everything is rigorously fixed by statute—what particular animal is to be offered in each species of sacrifice or on any given occasion ; its sex and age, and sometimes even its color ; its accompaniments and the precise ceremonies to be observed are specified. The whole has become a matter of ritual, an affair of the priests, who absorb as their perquisites what had previously fed the devotion of the offerer.

All this, and much beside, is urged as indicating the progressive development in the Israelitish institutions as represented in these codes, which are hence regarded as separated by long intervals of time. The fallacy lies in putting asunder what really belongs together. All belong to one comprehensive and harmonious body of law, though each separate portion has its own particular design, by which its form and contents are determined. That the Book of the Covenant is so brief and elementary in matters of worship is because of its preliminary character. It was intended simply to be the basis of God's covenant with Israel, not to develop in detail the duties growing out of that covenant relation. That Deuteronomy does not contain the minute ceremonial requirements to be found in Leviticus is no indication that the latter is the subsequent development of a more ritualistic age. It is simply because there was no need of repeating details which had already been sufficiently enlarged upon elsewhere. The Priest code was for the guidance of the priests, in conducting the ritual; Deuteronomy for the people at large, to whom the great lawgiver addressed his earnest warnings and exhortations as he was on the point of being taken from them. The differences and discrepancies alleged in these laws are for the most part capable of being satisfactorily harmonized. If a few

puzzles remain insoluble by us, they are not more than
might be expected in matters of so ancient date, so
foreign from modern ideas and usages and in regard to
which we are so imperfectly informed. If we had more
knowledge our present difficulties would doubtless vanish,
as others once considered formidable have long since dis-
appeared.

The Book of the Covenant, primitive as it is, nevertheless could not have been enacted in the desert; for it has
laws respecting fields and vineyards and olive-yards and
standing grain and grain in shocks (Ex. xxii. 5, 6; xxiii.
11), and offerings of first-fruits (xxii. 29, xxiii. 19), and six
years of tillage with a sabbatical year whose spontaneous
products should be for the poor and the beasts of the
field (xxiii. 10, 11), and harvest feasts and feasts of in-
gathering (xxiii.). All these have no application to a
people in the desert. They belong to a settled people,
engaged in agriculture. Such a law, it is alleged, could
only have been given after the settlement of the people
in Canaan.

The law of Deuteronomy, while greatly expanded beyond the Book of the Covenant in its provisions, has one
marked and characteristic feature which serves to define
the period to which it belongs. The Book of the Covenant (Ex. xx. 24), sanctions altars in all places where God
records his name. Deuteronomy, on the other hand (ch.
xii.), strictly limits the offering of sacrifice to the one
place which Jehovah should choose. Now, it is said, the
period of the judges and the early kings is marked by a
multiplicity of altars and worship in high places in accordance with the Book of the Covenant. But in the
reign of king Josiah, more than eight hundred years
after the settlement in Canaan, the high places were
abolished and sacrifice was restricted to the altar in Jerusalem. And this was done in obedience to the require-

ments of a book of the law then found in the temple (2 Kin. xxii. 8). That book was Deuteronomy. It was the soul of the entire movement. And this is the period to which it belongs.

This new departure, though successful so long as the pious Josiah lived, spent its force when he was taken away ; and under his ungodly successors the people relapsed again into the worship on high places, the popular attachment to which had not been eradicated. This was effectually broken, however, by the Babylonish captivity, which severed the people from the spots which they had counted sacred, until all the old associations had faded away. The returning exiles, impoverished and few in number, were bent only on restoring the temple in Jerusalem, and had no other place at which to worship. It was then and under these circumstances that Ezra came forth with a fresh book of law, adapted to the new state of things, and engaged the people to obedience (Neh. viii.). This book, then first produced, was the Ritual law or the Priest code. It also limits sacrifice to one place, as was done by Deuteronomy ; but in the latter this was regarded as a new departure, which it would be difficult to introduce, and which is, therefore, reiterated and insisted upon with great urgency (Deut. xii.). In the Priest code, on the contrary, it is quietly assumed as a matter of course, as though nothing else was thought of, and this had been the established rule from the time of Moses.

It had been customary for critics to attribute the Priest code to the Elohist, and the Book of the Covenant to the Jehovist ; so that the former was considered the first, and the latter the second legislation. Graf, who in his famous essay on the " Historical Books of the Old Testament," in 1866, undertook to reverse this order in the manner already indicated, felt it necessary to separate the historical from the legal portion of the Elohist document, and to maintain that, while the former was the oldest portion of the Pentateuch, the latter was the latest. It was promptly shown, however, in opposition to Graf, that such a separation was impossible. The connection between the Elohist histories and the ritual legislation was too intimate to be severed. Kuenen, Professor in Leyden, then boldly grasped the situation, accepted the order of the legislation proposed by Graf, and intrepidly contended, against the unanimous voice of all antecedent critics, that the entire Elohist document, history and legislation, was the latest constituent of the Pentateuch. This reversal of all former beliefs on this subject rendered necessary by the Development Hypothesis, met at first with determined opposition. It was not until 1878, seventeen years ago, that Julius Wellhausen assumed its advocacy in the first volume of his " History of Israel." His skilful presentation won for it a sudden popularity, and it has since been all the rage in Germany. Seventeen years of supremacy in that land of speculation is scarcely sufficient, however, to guarantee its permanence even there. The history of the past would rather lead one to expect that in no long time it will be replaced by some fresh novelty.[1]

[1] For further details in respect to the history of Pentateuch Criticism see the Nachwort, by Merx, to the second edition of Tuch's Commentar über die Genesis, pp. lxxviii.–cxxii.

Wellhausen's Übersicht über den Fortgang der Pentateuchkritik seit Bleek's Tode in Bleek's Einleitung in das Alte Testament, fourth edition, pp. 152–178.

Kuenen's Hexateuch (English Translation), Outline of the History of the Criticism of the Pentateuch and Book of Joshua during the last Quarter of a Century, pp. xi.–xl.

The following additional works may here be named, which are written in the interest of the Development Hypothesis :

Kayser: Das vorexilische Buch der Urgeschichte Israels und seine Erweiterungen, 1874.

This reversal of the order of the Elohist and the Jehovist at once put an end to the Supplement Hypothesis.

Wellhausen : Die Composition des Hexateuchs, in the Jahrbücher für Deutsche Theologie, 1876 and 1877 ; also reprinted separately in his Skizzen und Vorarbeiten, vol. ii.

Reuss : Geschichte der heiligen Schriften des Alten Testaments, 1881.

Cornill : Einleitung in das Alte Testament, 1891.

Holzinger : Einleitung in den Hexateuch, 1893.

Wildeboer : Die Litteratur des Alten Testaments, 1895.

The latest form of the partition of Genesis adopted by this school of critics is very conveniently exhibited to the eye by a diversity of type in Kantzsch und Socin, Die Genesis mit äusserer Unterscheidung der Quellenschriften, second edition, 1891. This is reproduced for English readers, in a diversity of colors, in Dr. E. C. Bissell's Genesis Printed in Colors, showing the original sources from which it is supposed to have been compiled, 1892. In B. W. Bacon's The Genesis of Genesis, 1892, the supposed documents are first indicated by a diversity of type, and then each is in addition printed separately.

This hypothesis is antagonized by Dillmann, in his Commentaries on the Pentateuch and Joshua, in one of its main positions, that the Priest code was posterior to Deuteronomy.

It was still more decidedly opposed by—

D. Hoffmann in a series of articles in the Magazin für die Wissenschaft des Judenthums, 1876–1880.

Franz Delitzsch in articles in Luthardt's Zeitschrift für Kirchliche Wissenschaft und Leben, 1880, 1882.

Bredenkamp : Gesetz und Propheten, 1881.

F. E. König : Die Hauptprobleme der israelitischen Religions geschichte, 1884.

E. König : Einleitung in das Alte Testament, 1893.

Also on still more thoroughly evangelical ground by—

A. Zahn : Das Deuteronomium, 1890.

E. Rupprecht : Das Rätsel des Fünfbuches Mose und seine falsche Lösung, 1894. Des Rätsels Lösung, 1895.

This hypothesis was introduced to the English public and advocated by—

W. Robertson Smith in several articles in the Encyclopædia Britannica, and in The Old Testament in the Jewish Church, 1881 ; second edition, 1892.

S. R. Driver: An Introduction to the Literature of the Old Testament, 1891.

C. A. Briggs : The Higher Criticism of the Hexateuch, 1893.

Among the replies made to it in Great Britain may be named—

R. Watts : The Newer Criticism and the Analogy of the Faith.

For the Jehovist could not have made additions to the
Elohist document if that document did not come into
existence until centuries after his time. It thus became
necessary to assume that the Jehovist passages, however
isolated and fragmentary, constituted a separate document; and the continuity was made out, as proposed by
Hupfeld, by using scattered clauses torn from their connection to bridge the chasms. The second Elohist of
Hupfeld also became a necessity, though now supposed
to antedate the first. The passages in the patriarchal
history alluded to by Hosea and other early prophets
must be eliminated from the Elohist document before
this can be reckoned postexilic. The great bulk of the
history is accordingly made over to the second Elohist,
and so this argument of early date is evaded. In this
manner the way is smoothed for turning all former con-

Deuteronomy the People's Book, its Origin and Nature (by J. Sime,
Esq., published anonymously), 1877.

J. Sime, Esq. : The Kingdom of All-Israel, 1883.

A. Cave : The Inspiration of the Old Testament, 1888.

Bishop Ellicott : Christus Comprobator, 1891.

J. Robertson : The Early Religion of Israel (Baird Lecture for 1889).

Lex Mosaica, or the Law of Moses and the Higher Criticism (Essays
by various writers), edited by R. V. French, 1894.

The following may be mentioned among those that have appeared in
America :

E. C. Bissell : The Pentateuch, its Origin and Structure, 1885.

G. Vos : The Mosaic Origin of the Pentateuchal Codes, 1886.

C. M. Mead : Christ and Criticism, 1892.

Essays on Pentateuchal Criticism, by various writers, edited by T. W.
Chambers, 1888.

Anti-Higher Criticism (articles by various writers), edited by L. W.
Munhall, 1894.

T. E. Schmauk : The Negative Criticism and the Old Testament, 1894.

F. R. Beattie : Radical Criticism, 1895.

W. H. Green : Moses and the Prophets, 1883. The Hebrew Feasts
in their Relation to Recent Critical Hypotheses, 1885.

The following able work in defence of the authorship of Moses and in
opposition to the development hypothesis has recently appeared in Hol-
land : Hoedemaker, De Mozaische Oorsprong van de Wetten in Exodus,
Leviticus en Numeri, 1895.

ceptions of the critics regarding the formation of the Pentateuch upside down. The Elohim document, from being the oldest and most reliable, becomes the latest and the least trustworthy. It is even charged that its facts are manufactured for a purpose; that the author makes statements not because he has evidence of their truth, but because they correspond with his ideas of what ought to have occurred, and what he therefore imagines must have occurred. Instead of representing the Mosaic age as it really was he gives, as Dr. Driver expresses it ("Literature of the O. T.," p. 120), "an ideal picture" of it.

SCRIPTURAL STATEMENTS.

It has already been remarked, as is indeed obvious upon its face, that the Development Hypothesis flatly contradicts throughout the account which the Pentateuch gives of itself. The laws are all explicitly declared to have been Mosaic, to have been written down by Moses, or to have been communicated to him directly from the LORD. And there is no good reason for discrediting the biblical statements on this subject. The three codes belong precisely where the Scripture narrative places them, and they are entirely appropriate in that position. The elementary character of the Book of the Covenant is explained not by its superior antiquity, but by its preliminary purpose. It was a brief body of regulations intended to serve as a basis for the formal ratification of the covenant between Jehovah and the people of Israel. Accordingly all that was required was a few simple and comprehensive rules, framed in the spirit of the religion of Jehovah, for the government of the people in their relations to one another and in their relation to God, to which in a solemn act of worship they were to pledge assent. After this fundamental act had been duly per-

formed, and the covenant relation had thus been instituted and acknowledged by both the contracting parties
the way was open for a fuller development of the duties
and obligations involved in this relation. Jehovah as
the covenant God of Israel would henceforth take up his
abode in the midst of his people. This made it necessary that detailed instructions should be given, for which
there was no occasion before, respecting the construction
of the sacred Tabernacle, the services to be performed in
it, the officiating priesthood, the set times for special
solemnities, and in general the entire ritual to be observed by a holy people for the expression and perpetu-
ation of their communion with a holy God. All this was
embodied in the Priest code, in which the scanty general
provisions of the Book of the Covenant regarding divine
worship were replaced by a vastly expanded and minutely
specified ceremonial. This was not a development implying the lapse of ages with an altered civilization and a corresponding advance in the popular notions of the Divine
Being, and of the homage that should be paid to him.

At the close of the forty years' wandering, when the
great legislator was about to die, he recapitulated in the
audience of the people the laws already given in the Book
of the Covenant, with such modifications and additions as
were suggested by the circumstances in which they were
placed, the experience of the past, and the prospects of
the immediate future. The Deuteronomic code thus enacted was a development, not as the Priest code had
been, on the side of the ritual, but considered as a code
for popular guidance in civil and religious matters. The
enlargement, which we here find, of the simple regulations of the Book of the Covenant implies no longer interval and no greater change in the condition or constitution of the people than is provided for in the Scripture
narrative. And at the same time the fact that we do not
10

find in Deuteronomy a ritual so elaborate and minutely detailed as in Leviticus, is not because Leviticus is the further development of a still later period, when ceremonies were more multiplied and held in higher esteem, but simply because Leviticus was a professional book, and Deuteronomy was a popular book. Leviticus was for the guidance of the priests who were professionally charged with the oversight and direction of the ceremonial, and Deuteronomy for the guidance of the people in matters more immediately within their province. Medical works for the instruction of physicians must necessarily be more minute than sanitary rules for popular use. And if it would be absurd to say that the same eminent physician could not produce both a professional and a popular treatise on medicine, it is equally so to insist, as the critics do, that Deuteronomy and Leviticus cannot both be from the same age and the same legislator.

It is further to be observed that the agricultural allusions in the Book of the Covenant are not in conflict with its Mosaic origin, and its delivery at Sinai. The people were on their way to Canaan. This land had been promised to their fathers, and the LORD had renewedly promised to give it to them. It was with this expectation that they left Egypt. For this they were marching through the desert. Canaan was their anticipated home, the goal of their hopes. They confidently trusted that they would soon be settled there in full possession. That there was to be even so much as a delay of forty years, and that the entire adult generation was to pass away before this hope was fulfilled, never entered the mind of the leader or the people ; since neither could have imagined such an act of gross rebellion as that for which they were sentenced to perish in the wilderness. It would have been strange, indeed, if the law given under these circumstances did not look beyond the desert as their abode, and took no note of what was in immediate prospect. It was quite appropriate for it to contemplate their expected life in Canaan, and to give regulations respecting the fields and vineyards and olive yards, which they were shortly to possess.

NO DISCREPANCY.

And there is no such difference as is pretended between the Book of the Covenant and the other Mosaic codes in respect to the place of legitimate sacrifice. It is not true that the former sanctioned a multiplicity of altars, and that this was the recognized practice of pious worshippers of Jehovah until the reign of Josiah, and that he instituted a new departure from all previous law and custom by restricting sacrifice to one central altar in compliance with a book of the law then for the first time promulgated. The unity of the altar was the law of Israel's life from the beginning. Even in the days of the patriarchs, Abraham, Isaac, and Jacob, no such thing was known as separate rival sanctuaries for the worship of Jehovah, coexisting in various parts of the land. They built altars and offered sacrifice in whatever part of the land they might be, particularly in places where Jehovah appeared to them. But the patriarchal family was a unit, and while they worshipped in different places successively in the course of their migrations, they nevertheless worshipped in but one place at a time. They did not offer sacrifice contemporaneously on different altars. So with Israel in their marches through the wilderness. They set up their altar wherever they encamped, at various places successively, but not in more than one place at the same time. This is the state of things which is recognized and made legitimate in the Book of the Covenant. In Exodus xx. 24, the Israelites are authorized to erect an altar, not wherever they may please, but "in all places where God records his name." The critics interpret this as a direct sanction given to various sanctuaries in different parts of Palestine. There is no foundation whatever for such an interpretation. There is not a word here nor anywhere in Scripture, from which the legitimacy of the multitudinous sanctuaries of a later time can be inferred. An altar is lawful, and sacrifice upon it acceptable, and God will there meet with his people and bless them only where he records his name; not where men may utter his name, whether by invocation or proclamation, but where God reveals or manifests himself. He manifested himself gloriously on Sinai amid awful indications of his presence. This was Moses's warrant for building an altar there (Ex. xxiv. 4). When the tabernacle was erected, and the ark deposited in it as the abiding symbol of the divine presence, that became the spot where God recorded his name, and to which all sacrifices were to be brought (Lev. xvii. 5). So that wherever the tabernacle or the ark was stationed, an altar might properly be erected and sacrifices offered.

And Deuteronomy xii. looks forward to the time when Israel should be permanently settled in the land which Jehovah their God was giving them to inherit, and he should have given them rest from all their enemies round about so that they should dwell in safety; then he would choose a place out of all their tribes to put his name there, and that should thenceforth be his habitation and the sole place of legitimate sacrifice. These conditions were not fulfilled until the peaceful reign of Solomon, who by divine direction built the temple as Jehovah's permanent abode. Here the Most High placed his name by filling it with his effulgent glory at its dedication, and thenceforward this was the one place whither the people went up to meet with God and worship him by sacrifice;

thither they directed their prayers, and from his holy hill of Zion God sent forth his help and his salvation.

There is thus the most entire concord between the several codes in regard to the place of sacrifice. It was from the beginning limited to the place of divine manifestation. As this manifestation was on all ordinary occasions restricted first to the Mosaic tabernacle, and then to the temple of Solomon, the language of the Book of the Covenant no less than that of the Levitical and Deuteronomic codes demanded that sacrifice should ordinarily be restricted to these sacred edifices. Only the Book of the Covenant, which lays down the primal and universal law of the Hebrew altar, is wider in its scope, inasmuch as it embraces those extraordinary occasions likewise for which there was no need to make express provision in the other codes. If God manifested himself by an immediate and supernatural appearance elsewhere than at the sanctuary, that spot became, not permanently indeed, but so long as the manifestation lasted, holy ground, and a place of legitimate sacrifice. And on the other hand, if the Most High at any time withdrew his ordinary presence from the sanctuary, as when the ark was captured by the Philistines, the sanctuary ceased to be the place where God recorded his name, the restriction of sacrifice to that spot was, *ipso facto*, for the time abolished; and in the absence of any definite provision for the regular seat of God's worship, the people were left to offer sacrifice as best they might. To the extent of these two exceptional cases the Book of the Covenant is more comprehensive than the other codes. But it lends no sanction whatever to that irregular and unregulated worship which the critics would make it cover.

After the capture of the ark, and during the period of its seclusion in a private house which followed, the worship on high places had a certain sort of legitimacy from the exigencies of the situation, as is expressly stated (1 Kin. iii. 2); as it had also at a later period in the apostate kingdom of Israel, where the pious among the people were restrained from going to the house of God in Jerusalem. But apart from these exceptional cases worship at other altars than that at the sanctuary was in violation of the express statute.

ALLEGED VIOLATIONS OF THE LAW.

The critics argue the non-existence of the law from its repeated violation. It is claimed that the history shows that the laws of the Pentateuch were not in fact obeyed: whence it is inferred that no such laws were then known. It is admitted, of course, that there were numerous departures from God and repeated open violations or continued neglect of his laws. The history records such instances again and again, but it brands them in every case as wilful transgressions against God and his known law. It does not follow from the perpetration of murder and theft that such acts were not regarded as criminal, nor that the sixth and eighth commandments were unknown. When it is over and over charged that the people forsook the LORD and worshipped Baal and Ashtaroth, this can be explained in no other way than as an apostasy from Jehovah to these foreign deities. For if there is anything that is obvious, it is that Jehovah was Israel's God from the beginning. Such open declensions from the true God have no bearing, therefore, on the present subject. They were plain offences against known and acknowledged obligation.

But it is affirmed that good men at different periods acted habitually at variance with the requirement of the ritual laws without incurring censure and apparently without being sensible that they were doing wrong or transgressing any commandment.

Thus, while the law required that sacrifices should be offered only at the sanctuary and only by priests, the sons of Aaron, repeated mention is made of sacrifices being offered to the LORD, and, so far as appears, with acceptance, though it was elsewhere than at the sanctuary, and the offerer was not a descendant of Aaron. Thus the children of Israel offered sacrifice at Bochim (Judg. ii. 5), in a penitential spirit when rebuked for their neglects of duty by the angel of the LORD. Gideon built two altars in Ophrah and offered a bullock upon one of them to the LORD (Judg. vi. 24–27). Manoah offered a kid in sacrifice upon a rock to the LORD (Judg. xiii. 19). This it is said, is in direct violation of the law of Deuteronomy xii. 6, 13, 14, Numbers xviii. 7, though it accords with the prescriptions of the Book of the Covenant, which recognizes no separate order of priests, and permits sacrifices (Ex. xx. 24), in all places where the LORD records his name. It is hence inferred that the laws of Deuteronomy and the Priest code were not in existence, but only the Book of the Covenant.

It has already been shown, however, that there is no variance between these laws in respect to the place of sacrifice ; and the Aaronic priesthood was not yet instituted when the Book of the Covenant was framed. The sacrifices at Bochim, and those that were offered by Gideon and Manoah are readily accounted for by the extraordinary circumstances that called them forth. On all ordinary occasions the sanctuary was the place for sacrificial worship and this was to be offered only by the priests, who were specially charged with this service. But when God manifested himself in an extraordinary manner in any place remote from the tabernacle, that place became for the time a sanctuary, and the person to whom he thus manifested himself became for the time a priest. The special prerogative of the priest is that he is authorized to "come near" unto God, Num. iii. 10, xvi. 5, 40, Ezek. xliv. 15, 16; he, to whom God visibly appears and thus brings him near to himself, is accordingly invested temporarily with a sacerdotal character. God must be worshipped wherever he appeared, and by whomsoever he honored by such special manifestation. Accordingly, whenever throughout the book of Judges the LORD or the angel of the LORD appeared to men, they offered sacrifice on the spot; and no sacrifices were offered elsewhere than at the sanctuary or by any other than a priest, except upon the occasion of such a special manifestation of the divine presence.

It is further to be observed that sacrifices might be offered anywhere in the presence of the ark of the covenant. The ark was the symbol of the LORD's presence. It was the ark in the tabernacle which made the latter a holy place. And when the ark was taken from the tabernacle, it was still the throne of God, who dwelt between the cherubim. Wherever the ark was, there was the symbol of God's presence; and hence when the ark was present at Bethel (Judg. xx. 26, 27), or when it came back from the Philistines to Beth-shemesh (1 Sam. vi. 14), sacrifices were offered to the LORD. And so when David was transporting the ark to Zion, oxen and fatlings were sacrificed before it (2 Sam. vi. 13).

But we find the prophet Samuel offering sacrifice (1 Sam. vii. 9, 17) away from the ark and the tabernacle, and without any special divine manifestation having been made. This was again because of the peculiar circumstances of the case. In consequence of the sins of Eli's sons, and in general the wickedness of both priests and people, God suffered the sacred ark to be taken captive by the Philistines. The removal of the symbol of his presence was significant of God's forsaking Shiloh and forsaking his people (Ps. lxxviii. 59–61, 67, 68; Jer. vii.

12; xxvi. 6, 9). The Philistines were compelled by the heavy plagues sent upon them to return the ark. But the ark was not taken back to Shiloh, which the LORD had so signally rejected as his abode. It was hid away in the seclusion of a private house until the favor of the LORD should again return to his people. God had abandoned the sanctuary, and there was thenceforth no legitimate sanctuary in Israel until the ark was taken to Zion and the LORD chose that for his abode. During this period, when Israel was without a divinely sanctioned sanctuary, Samuel, as God's prophet and representative, by divine authority, assumed the functions of the degenerate priesthood, and sacrifices were offered on high places. This state of things continued, as we are told (1 Kin. iii. 2), until the temple of Solomon was built, when that became God's dwelling-place; and as that was the spot which God had chosen to place his name there, (1 Kin. viii. 29), it henceforth was the only lawful place of sacrifice. We do indeed read after that of offerings made on high places, but they were illegal and were regarded as such, and pious princes endeavored to suppress them, with varying success, until at last Hezekiah, and more effectually still, Josiah, succeeded in abolishing them.

It is confessed, accordingly, that sacrifices were in repeated instances offered elsewhere than at the sanctuary; but whether these were justified by extraordinary circumstances, or whether they were irregular and condemned as such, they cannot disprove the existence of the law restricting sacrifice to one common altar in all ordinary cases.

IGNORANCE OF THE LAW.

Still further, some infractions of the law may be attributable to ignorance of its requirements. Moses directed that the law should be publicly read every seventh year,

Deut. xxxi. 10–13. Teaching the people its statutes was at all times the special duty of the priests, Lev. x. 11, Deut. xxiv. 8, Mal. ii. 7, and of the Levites, Deut. xxxiii. 10. But in periods of declension it may easily be supposed this duty was neglected, and that priests and Levites themselves may have been as ignorant of the law as monks of the Middle Ages were of the Bible, 1 Sam. ii. 12, 13 (marg. Rev. Ver.), Hos. iv. 6. Precepts of the law long disregarded would fade from the memory of the people. Mingling with idolaters they adopted their customs and were infected with their ideas to such an extent that Jephthah could even sacrifice his daughter to Jehovah in fulfilment of his vow, Judg. xi. 35.

My friend, Professor Zenos, of McCormick Theological Seminary, has directed my attention to the following signal instance in modern times of the total oblivion of a noted code of laws previously in force. It is thus described by Sir J. Stephen in his "Lectures on the History of France," Lecture IV., p. 94: "When the barbarism of the domestic government (under the Carlovingian dynasty) had thus succeeded the barbarism of the government of the state, one of the most remarkable results of that political change was the disappearance of the laws and institutions by which Charlemagne had endeavored to elevate and civilize his subjects. Before the close of the century in which he died the whole body of his laws had fallen into utter disuse throughout the whole extent of his Gallic dominions. They who have studied the charters, laws, and chronicles of the later Carlovingian princes most diligently are unanimous in declaring that they indicate either an absolute ignorance or an entire forgetfulness of the legislation of Charlemagne." Will the critics apply the same rule to Charlemagne that they do to Moses, and infer that he never gave the laws attributed to him?

It has been maintained on such grounds as have now been recited, that the law of Deuteronomy was unknown until the time of king Josiah ; that the worship on high places continued until his reign—that the prophetic and priestly party then became convinced in consequence of the idolatrous taint which infected the worship on high places, and the abuses and excesses prevalent there that the purity of religion demanded that they should be abolished and sacrifice restricted to the temple at Jerusalem. Accordingly the book of Deuteronomy, which strenuously insists upon the overthrow of the high places and the confining of sacrifice to the place which the LORD should choose, was prepared with the view of legalizing this measure and paving the way for its enforcement. This was attributed to Moses in order to give it a higher sanction. A copy was deposited in the temple, where it was found, as it was intended that it should be, by Hilkiah, the high-priest, and taken to the king, who carried the projected reform into effect (2 Kin. xxii. 8 ff.). Others, who are more reverential, seek to explain the discovery of the book and its enforcement as the work of Moses without involving fraud, but with very indifferent success.

The Priest code, it is alleged, is later still. That was the work of Ezra, and was prepared with reference to the needs of the period after the exile, and the ritualistic spirit which then prevailed. This is the book of the law produced by Ezra the scribe and read to the people, as recorded in Nehemiah viii., to which they solemnly engaged to render obedience. This code, however, it is contended, was not complete even in the days of Ezra. Additions were subsequently made to it, and continued to be made for some time thereafter. The day of atonement is not mentioned in either Ezra or Nehemiah, and its peculiar services were introduced at a later date. The altar of incense, with the special sacredness attached to the offering of incense, indicates, it is said, one of the later strata of the Priest code. And from some peculiarities in the Greek and Samaritan text of the description of the Mosaic tabernacle, it is confidently affirmed that changes and alterations in the Hebrew text continued to be made until after the time when those versions were prepared.

This whole theory of the successive origin and gradual growth of the different codes of the Pentateuchal law is not only directly in the face of the explicit statements of the Pentateuch itself, but is utterly inconsistent with the history on which it is professedly based. Both the book found in the temple in the reign of Josiah and that brought forward and read by Ezra after the exile, are expressly declared to have been not recent productions but the law of Moses. The assumption that laws were fraudulently attributed to the great legislator is gratuitous and without foundation. The idea that such a fraud could be successfully perpetrated is preposterous. It is utterly out of the question that a body of laws never before heard of could be imposed upon the people as though they had been given by Moses centuries before, and that they could have been accepted and obeyed by them, notwithstanding the fact that they imposed new and serious burdens, set aside established usages to which the people were devotedly attached, and conflicted with the interests of numerous and powerful classes of the people. And it further involves the incongruity of assuming that three codes, which were at variance in their provisions, the first having been superseded by the second, and the second in turn superseded by the third, came subsequently to be regarded as entirely harmonious, and as one body of law which had been united from the beginning and was all alike obligatory.

VI

THE BEARING OF THE DIVISIVE CRITICISM ON THE CREDIBILITY OF THE PENTATEUCH AND ON SUPERNATURAL RELIGION

IT is noteworthy that the partition hypotheses in all their forms have been elaborated from the beginning in the interest of unbelief. The unfriendly animus of an opponent does not indeed absolve us from patiently and candidly examining his arguments, and accepting whatever facts he may adduce, though we are not bound to receive his perverted interpretation of them. Nevertheless we cannot intelligently nor safely overlook the palpable bias against the supernatural which has infected the critical theories which we have been reviewing, from first to last. All the acknowledged leaders of the movement have, without exception, scouted the reality of miracles and prophecy and immediate divine revelation in their genuine and evangelical sense. Their theories are all inwrought with naturalistic presuppositions, which cannot be disentangled from them without their falling to pieces. Evangelical scholars in Germany, as elsewhere, steadfastly opposed these theories, refuted the arguments adduced in their support, and exposed their malign tendencies. It is only recently that there has been an attempt at compromise on the part of certain believing scholars, who are disposed to accept these critical theories and endeavor to harmonize them with the Christian faith. But the inherent vice in these systems cannot be eradicated. The inevitable result has been to lower the

Christian faith to the level of these perverted theories instead of lifting the latter up to the level of a Christian standard.

CREDIBILITY UNDERMINED.

According to the critical hypothesis, even in the most moderate hands, the situation is this: The Pentateuch, instead of being one continuous and self-consistent history from the pen of Moses, is made up of four distinct documents which have been woven together, but which the critics claim that they are able to separate and restore, as far as the surviving remnants of each permit, to their original condition. These severally represent the traditions of the Mosaic age as they existed six, eight, and ten centuries after the Exodus.[1] When these are compared they are found to be in perpetual conflict. Events wear an entirely different complexion in one from that which they have in another; the characters of those who appear in them, the motives by which they are actuated, and the whole impression of the period in which they live is entirely different.

It is very evident from all this why the critics tell us that the doctrine of inspiration must be modified. If these Pentateuchal documents, as they describe them, were inspired, it must have been in a very peculiar sense. It is not a question of inerrancy, but of wholesale mutual contradiction which quite destroys their credit as truthful histories. And these contradictions, be it observed, are not in the Pentateuch itself, but result from the mangling and the mal-interpretations to which it has been subjected by the critics.

On the critical hypothesis the real facts of the history

---

[1] J and E are commonly referred to the eighth or ninth century B.C.; D to the reign of Josiah or shortly before it; P to the period after the Babylonish exile.

are not what they seem to be to the ordinary reader. They can only be elicited by an elaborate critical process. The several documents must first be disentangled and carefully compared; the points in which they agree and those in which they differ must be noted. And from this conflicting mass of testimony the critic must ascertain, as best he may, how much can be relied upon as true, how much has a certain measure of probability, and how much must be rejected altogether.

Another element of precariousness enters into the critical attempts to distinguish what is reliable from what is not, in the Pentateuchal narratives. By the confession of the critics themselves, and by the necessity of their hypothesis, the documents which they fancy that they have discovered are by no means complete. By singling out the paragraphs and clauses which are regarded as belonging to each of the documents severally, and putting them together, they undertake the reconstruction of the original documents, which are supposed in the first instance to have circulated separately as distinct and independent publications, but to have been subsequently fused together into the Pentateuch, as we now possess it, by a series of redactors. First, the two oldest documents, J and E, were combined, and the combination was effected, it is supposed, by the following method: sections or paragraphs, longer or shorter, were taken alternately from J and from E, and pieced together so as to form one continuous narrative. It was the purpose of the redactor to make the best use that he possibly could of these two sources at his command in preparing a history of the period of which they treat. In some cases he made full extracts from both his sources of all that they contained, and preserved the language of each unaltered, making no additions or modifications of his own. Frequently, however, it was necessary to adjust what was thus taken from different works, in order to make it read smoothly, or to render it harmonious. Hence, upon occasion he introduced explanatory remarks, or made such changes as seemed to be required in what he borrowed from J or from E. Sometimes his sources were so nearly parallel that it would lead to needless repetition to use them both. In such cases, accordingly, he confined himself to the account given in one of the documents, either omitting the corresponding statements of the other altogether, or weaving in a clause or a sentence here and there when it seemed to him distinctive and important. Again, cases occur in which the narratives of J and E were in real or apparent conflict. Here he does the best that he can. He either undertakes to harmonize their accounts, where this is possible, by inserting some statement which seems to reconcile them, by so changing the order of the narrative as to relieve the difficulty, or by converting inconsistent accounts of the same event into two different transactions. Where none of these methods is practicable, and reconciliation is out of the question, the redactor adheres to one of his sources and disregards the other.

D, which was composed some time after this union of JE, existed for a while as an independent work, and was then combined with JE by a new redactor, who, besides attaching D to this previously existing work, retouched JE in several places, and introduced a number of passages from his own point of view, which was different from that of the older historians.

Finally the document P was prepared, at first as a separate publication, but at length it was interwoven by a third redactor with the pre-existing triplicate treatise JED, the process being substantially the same as has already been described in the case of JE.

This is in general the method by which the critics suppose that the Pentateuch was gradually brought to its present form.   It will be seen at a glance how the complexity of the critical problem is increased by the successive editorial labors which are supposed to have been brought into requisition in the course of the construction of the Pentateuch.   The several documents must not only be distinguished from each other, but also from the various redactional additions and insertions which have at any time been made.

Let us assume that this delicate and difficult analysis has been effected with unfailing accuracy notwithstanding the liabilities to error vitiating the result, which increase at every step.   But waiving this, what is the situation when the analysis has been accomplished ? and what is its bearing upon the historical character of the Pentateuch ?

The critics have undertaken to reproduce for us the documents J, E, D, and P, which are our primary sources for both the Mosaic and the patriarchal history, and which date respectively six, eight, and ten centuries after the Exodus.   These documents are not only at variance with each other in their statements respecting numerous particulars, thus invalidating each other's testimony and showing that the traditions which they have severally followed are mutually inconsistent ; but they are besides very incomplete.   Numerous gaps and omissions occur in each.   Matter which they once contained, as is evident from allusions still found in them, is now missing ; how much it is impossible to tell.

But what is more serious, the parts that yet remain have been manipulated by the various redactors.   The order of events has been disturbed ; events really distinct have been confused and mistaken for one and the same ; and narratives of the same event have been mistaken for events altogether distinct ; statements which are mislead-

11

ing have been inserted with the view of harmonizing what cannot in fact be reconciled; when traditions vary, instead of being recorded in their integrity to afford some opportunity of ascertaining the truth by comparison, they have either been mingled together, thus disturbing both, or one only has been preserved, thus leaving no check upon its inaccuracies. All this and more, the critics tell us, the several redactors have done with their materials. No charge is made of dishonest intentions. But surely it is most unfortunate for the historical value of their work. There is no way of ascertaining how far these materials have been warped from their proper orig-inal intent by the well-meant but mistaken efforts of the redactors to correct or to harmonize them. That their meaning has been seriously altered in repeated instances, which are pointed out by the critics, creates a very natural presumption that like changes have been freely made elsewhere which can now no longer be detected.

It is difficult to understand in what sense the redac-tors, whose work has been described, can be said to have been inspired. They certainly had no inspiration which preserved them from error, or even from making the gravest historical mistakes. They had no such inspira-tion as gives any divine attestation to their work. The Pentateuchal history gathers no confirmation from having passed through their hands.

Upon the theory of the most conservative of the divi-sive critics, for it is this with which we have been deal-ing, what dependence can be placed upon the historical statements of the Pentateuch ? These are, as they allege, inaccurate and inconsistent with themselves not in the patriarchal period merely, but throughout the lifetime of Moses, when the foundation was laid of the Old Testa-ment religion and those signal miracles were wrought which gave it undeniable divine sanction. The real facts are not those which appear upon the surface. They can only be elicited by an elaborate critical process which shall detect and remove the mistaken additions and attempted emendations of each of the redactors, and shall then restore the four documents to their pristine condition, so far as what remains of each will allow. This will put the critic in possession of a mutilated record of four variant traditions of the Mosaic age, as these existed six, eight, and ten centuries after that date. And now it is by the help of such materials in the way of comparison, correction, and elimination that he must sift out and ascertain the real facts. Must we not say that the history of the Mosaic age, if this be the only way of arriving at it, rests upon a quicksand? and that nothing of any consequence can be certainly known regarding it?

Here is no question merely of the strict inerrancy of Scripture, of absolute accuracy in unimportant minutiæ, of precision in matters of science. This is not the issue raised by the theorizing of that class of biblical critics with which we contend. And it is no mere question of the mode of inspiration. But it is the question whether any dependence can be placed upon the historical truth of the Bible; whether our confidence in the facts recorded in the Pentateuch rests upon any really trustworthy basis; facts, be it observed, not of mere scientific or antiquarian interest, but which mark the course of God's revelations to the patriarchs and to Moses. It is the certainty of facts which are vital to the religion of the Old Testament, and the denial of whose truth weakens the foundations on which the New Testament itself is built. The critical theory which we have been examining is destructive of all rational certainty of the reality of these truths; and thus tends to overturn the historical basis of the religion of the Bible.

UNFRIENDLY TO REVEALED RELIGION

It is no merely literary question, then, which this style of criticism raises. It is not simply whether the Pentateuch was written by one author or another, while its historic truth and its divine authority remain unaffected. The truth and evidence of the entire Mosaic history are at stake. And with this stands or falls the reality of God's revelation to Moses and the divine origin of the Old Testament. And this again is not only vouched for and testified to by our divine Lord and Saviour Jesus Christ and his inspired apostles, but upon this the Lord Jesus bases his own claims. Moses wrote of him. The predictions uttered and recorded by Moses speak of Christ. The types, of which both the Pentateuchal history and the Mosaic institutions are full, point to Christ. But if the predictions are not genuine, and the history is untrue, and the institutions were not ordained of God, but are simply the record of priestly usage, what becomes of the witness which they bear to Christ? And must not the religion of the Old Testament sink in our esteem from a religion directly revealed of God to one which is the outgrowth of the Israelitish mind and heart, under an uplifting influence from above, it may be, but still proceeding from man, not from God? It is then based not on positive truth authoritatively communicated from God to man, but on the aspirations and reflections, the yearnings and longings and spiritual struggles of devout and holy men seeking after God, with such divine guidance and inward illumination as good men in every age may enjoy, but that is all. There is no direct revelation, no infallible inspiration, no immediate and positive disclosure of the mind and will of God.

The religion of the Bible is not merely one of abstract doctrines respecting God. It does not consist merely in

monotheism, nor in right notions of the being and perfections of God as abstract truths. Nor does it consist
merely in devout emotions and aspirations toward the
Divine Being. But both its doctrines and its practical
piety are based on positive disclosures which God has
made of himself in his dealings with men and his communications to them. It is a historical religion based
on palpable outstanding facts, in which God has manifested himself, and by which he has put himself in living relation to men. Appeal is throughout made to the
mighty deeds and the great wonders wrought by his
uplifted hand and his outstretched arm in evidence that
it is the almighty God who has acted and spoken and
revealed himself, and no mere human imaginings. To
discredit these biblical statements is to discredit the
biblical revelation. And this is what is done throughout the entire Mosaic period, not by Kuenen and Wellhausen and Stade and Cornill merely, who are avowed
unbelievers in a supernatural revelation, but by those
likewise who claim to be evangelical critics.

It is notorious that the long succession of distinguished
scholars, by whom the divisive hypothesis has been elaborated in its application to the Pentateuch, have been unbelievers in an immediate supernatural revelation. And
they have not hesitated to avow their want of faith in the
reality of prophetic foresight and of miraculous powers.
The ready method by which these have been set aside
is by dexterous feats of criticism. Revelations of truth
and duty are brought down to such a period in the history as may fit in with some imagined naturalistic scheme
of development. Predictions which have been too accurately fulfilled to be explained away as vague anticipa-
tions, shrewd calculations, or lucky guesses, must, as
they claim, have been uttered, or at least committed to
writing, after the event. Miracles cannot have been

recorded by eye-witnesses or contemporaries, but are regarded as legendary exaggerations of events that are entirely explicable from natural causes. It is therefore assumed that they necessarily imply a sufficient interval between the occurrence and the written narrative to account for the growth of the story. A hypothesis wrought out on the basis of these principles, which are throughout covertly assumed, and the critical phenomena most ingeniously adjusted into conformity with them, can lead to no other result than that with reference to which it was shaped from the beginning. While the discussion seemingly turns on words and phrases and the supposed peculiarities of individual writers, the bent of the whole thing is to rivet the conclusion which the framers of the hypothesis have tacitly though steadily contemplated, a conclusion irrefragable on their philosophical principles, viz., that the supernatural must be eliminated from the Scriptures. And hence the hypothesis is at this time one of the most potent weapons in the hands of unbelief. Supernatural facts, which stand unshaken in the Mosaic records like granite mountains, impregnable to all other methods of attack, dissolve like wax in the critics' crucible.

Real discoveries are not, of course, to be discredited because of false principles that are entertained by the discoverers, or wrong motives that may have influenced them. If unbelievers in divine inspiration by their learned investigations can assist us in the elucidation or more correct appreciation of the sacred writings in any respect, we welcome their aid with all our hearts. But all is not gold that glitters. And there can be no impropriety in subjecting novelties to careful scrutiny, before we adopt conclusions at war with our most cherished convictions and with what we hold to be well-established truths. The apostle's maxim applies here, "Prove all things; hold fast that which is good." The recent acceptance of this hypothesis by men of high standing in evangelical circles does not rob it of the pernicious tendencies inwrought in its whole texture, and will not prevent the full development of these tendencies, if it shall ever gain prevalence.

One very momentous consequence of the adoption of this hypothesis is palpable upon its surface. It nullifies at once the Mosaic authorship of the Pentateuch, and substitutes anonymous documents of late age in an imperfect state of preservation, which have been woven together, and to some extent modified, by anonymous redactors. It is at once obvious what a vast diminution hence results in the external guarantee of the truth of the record. If Moses himself committed to writing the events in which he bore so conspicuous a part, and the laws and institutions enacted by him, and this product of Moses's own pen has been preserved to us in the Pentateuch, we have a voucher of the very first order of the accuracy of the narrative, in every particular, proceeding as it does not only from a contemporary and eye-witness cognizant of every detail, but from the leader and legislator whose genius shaped all that he records, and who was more than any other interested in its true and faithful transmission.

It would be a relief if these anonymous sources were the work of contemporaries and participants in the events recorded. If, as Delitzsch assumed when he first suffered himself to be captivated by the hypothesis, Eleazar or Joshua, or men of like stamp with them, were the authors of the documents, and these were put together in the age immediately succeeding that of Moses, it might seem as though this would afford abundant assurance of the truth of their statements. But who is to assure us that Eleazar or any of his compeers had a hand in these records?

If we abandon the Mosaic authorship, which is so explicitly and repeatedly certified by the earliest tradition that we are able to summon, we are out upon the open sea with nothing to direct our course. Nothing can disprove its composition by Moses which does not disprove its origin in the Mosaic age. All thought of its proceeding from the pen of contemporaries must then be abandoned. We go blindly groping along the centuries in quest of authors. All is unwarranted conjecture; there is no firm lodgement anywhere. The notion that the authors of these so-called documents, or the redactors who compiled the Pentateuch from them, can be identified in the absence of any ancient testimony pointing to another than Moses is utterly groundless.

But if the authors of the several documents were infallibly inspired, and if the redactors were likewise divinely guarded from error, would we not then have a perfectly trustworthy record, as much so though it were produced in a comparatively late age, as if it had been contemporaneous with the events themselves? This fond fancy is dispelled the moment we come to examine the actual working of the hypothesis, as this has been abundantly exhibited in the preceding pages. It is constructed on the assumption not merely of the fallibility but the falsity of the documents, whose accounts are represented to be not merely divergent but contradictory; upon the assumption likewise of the incompetency of the redactors, even if they are charged with nothing worse. They misunderstand their authorities, and, to say the least, unintentionally pervert them, ascribing to them a meaning foreign to their original and proper intent. The Pentateuch is thus held to be based upon conflicting narratives, written several centuries after the occurrences which they profess to relate, and embodying the diverse traditions which had meanwhile grown up respecting them.

These the redactors have undertaken to harmonize, though they were, so the critics affirm, mutually inconsistent. They have done this by rearrangements and additions of their own that obscure and alter their real meaning. The critics accordingly tell us that the Pentateuch on its face yields a very incorrect representation of what actually took place in the time to which it relates. The only way to reach the real facts is to undo the work of the redactors, eliminate their misleading additions, and restore, as far as possible, the documents to the condition in which they were before they were meddled with. This will put us in possession of the discordant traditions which had arisen in the course of centuries respecting the events in question. The comparison of these traditions will yield a modicum of truth upon the subject, and the rest must be left to conjecture.

And this, be it remembered, is a part of the canon of Scripture, the part, in fact, which lies at the foundation of the whole, that Scripture, which according to our blessed Lord cannot be broken, and which according to the apostle Paul is given by inspiration of God. Is it surprising that they who accept this hypothesis insist that the current doctrine of Scripture and of divine inspiration requires revision ?

The extent to which the Mosaic history crumbles away under such treatment as has been illustrated above, varies with different critics. To Kuenen and Wellhausen it is utterly untrustworthy. Others recoil from such unsparing demolition, and allow more or less to stand unchallenged. But this difference of result is due to the subjective state of the critic himself, not to any clear and intelligible ground in the nature of the case. The whole process is vicious. The claim is preposterous that a consistent and continuous narrative may be rent apart *ad libitum,* and meanings assigned to isolated portions, which the words might admit if viewed independently, but which are impossible in the connection. Yet this lies for the most part at the basis of the divisive criticism, determines generally the line of fracture, and imparts to the whole subject nearly all of its interest and importance in the view of its adherents. Even if the partition hypothesis were well founded and the documents, of which the critics speak so confidently, had a real and separate existence, the redactors who had them in their original completeness were much more competent to judge of their true meaning than modern critics, who by their own confession possess them only in a fragmentary and mutilated condition, and so blended together that it is extremely difficult, and often quite impossible, to disentangle them with certainty and accuracy. Under these circumstances to deal with the Pentateuch in its present form in a manner which implies either mistake or misrepresentation on the part of the redactors is gratuitous and inadmissible unless on the clearest and most unmistakable evidence.

It is nevertheless a fundamental assumption in the literary partition of the Pentateuch, that the redactors have misunderstood or misrepresented their sources; that narratives, which were but varying accounts of the same thing, were supposed by them to relate to distinct occurrences, and they have treated them as such, wrongly assigning them to different occasions and perhaps different persons; that they have combined their sources in such a way as to give a wrong coloring to their contents, so that they make a false impression and convey a meaning quite different from that which properly belonged to them in their original connection. And the chief value and interest of the critic is thought to be the new light which he brings into the narrative and the altered meaning which he discovers by undoing the work of the redactors, who are supposed to have cut away much precious material from their documents that is now irrecoverably lost, and to have modified even the mutilated remnant which they have handed down to us. Unless this be so, what is gained by the partition? If everything means just what it did before, what good has been accomplished? If, on the other hand, the meaning has been altered, the question returns, Which is right and which is the better entitled to our confidence, the redactors who had ample means of knowing what they were doing, or the modern critic who relies upon his conjectures for his facts?

A yet more serious aspect of this literary partition is that there is no limit to it. If the door be opened even on a crack to admit it, all is at the mercy of what there is no means of controlling; and nothing can prevent the door being flung as wide open as the hinges will allow. The appetite for division and subdivision grows by every concession made to quiet it. The analysis of Wellhausen, of Dillmann, of Jülicher, and of Stade shows that we have not yet reached the beginning of the end. Fresh seams are constantly discovered in what critics themselves have previously regarded as indivisible; fresh errors and mistakes are discovered in the narrative that were never suspected before; and the whole becomes the plaything of the critic's fancy. The advocates of literary partition among us at present may stand on comparatively conservative ground under the influence of their own past training and of cherished principles, which they are unwilling to abandon. But what is to hinder their followers, who are not similarly anchored, from pursuing this partition to its legitimate consequences? It is the first step that costs. And the initial step in this partition is the admission of the untrustworthiness of the sacred record as it now stands, and the necessity of transposition, alteration, and reconstruction in order to reach the real truth. After this initial admission has been made, everything further is but a question of degrees. The Scripture is no longer reliable in its present form. The inspiration of its writers has been surrendered. We have lost our infallible guide. And distrust may be carried to any length that the inward disposition of the operator inclines him to indulge it. In yielding the principle everything has been conceded that is involved in it and follows from it. The avalanche cannot be arrested midway in its descent.

The Pentateuch in its unity and integrity is impregnable to hostile assaults. But accept the partition of it which the critics offer, and the truth and inspiration of this portion of Holy Scripture no longer rest upon any solid basis.

DEISM, RATIONALISM, DIVISIVE CRITICISM.

The study of the Bible on its purely literary side has many and strong attractions for men of letters. It records the history and the institutions of a most remarkable people. It gives an insight into their character and usages, into their domestic, social, and political life; particularly it exhibits their religion in its spirit and its outward forms, a religion altogether unique in the ancient world, and the influence of which has been deep and wide-spread in later times. It contains all that has been preserved of their literary products through a long series of ages, including narratives of tender and touching interest, of deeds of heroic valor, of wise administration, of resolute adherence to right and duty under trying circumstances; poetic effusions of rare beauty, of exalted genius, on the most elevated themes, wise sayings, the utterance of sages or embodying profound and extensive observation ; the discourses of the prophets, haranguing kings and people in great critical conjunctures with impassioned patriotism and the noblest impulses, inculcating and enforcing the loftiest principles of action. There is much in all this to stir the enthusiasm and excite the interest of those who are engaged in literary pursuits.

It is not strange, then, that in the revival of letters, when the stores of ancient learning were thrown open to the gaze of the modern world, and men sat delighted before the masterpieces of Greece and Rome and the Orient, they should be charmed likewise by the fascinations of Hebrew literature. Scholars were drawn with equal relish to the songs of Horace, of Pindar, and of David ; they listened admiringly alike to the eloquent and burning words of Cicero, Demosthenes, and Isaiah. The Bible was scanned with avidity as the extant body of Israel's literature ; just that and nothing more. It was a most engaging study. It was expounded and illustrated and commented on from professors' chairs and in numerous volumes, precisely as the works of historians, poets, philosophers, and orators of other lands. But, with all the admiration that was bestowed upon it, the unique character of its claims was lost sight of. Its inspiration and divine authority did not enter into the account. The immediate voice and hand of God, which rule in the whole, were overlooked.

It is easy to see how the study of the Bible thus pursued would necessarily be warped. Treated as a purely human product, it must be reduced to the level of that which it was esteemed to be. The supernatural must be eliminated from it, since it was regarded as the resultant of purely human forces. And stripped of the supernatural, the Bible becomes a totally different book. There are three evident indications of God's immediate presence, which pervade the Scriptures from beginning to end, and are inwrought into its entire structure, and with which they must reckon who recognize in its contents merely that which is natural and human. These are miracle, prophecy, and revealed truth. The pages of the Bible are ablaze with recorded facts involving the immediate exercise of almighty power, with predictive utterances unveiling the future hid from mortal view, and with disclosures which quite transcend the reach of the human faculties. No man can undertake the study of the Bible, however superficially, without encountering these, which are among its most prominent features. And if it is to be comprehended from a naturalistic point of view, they must in some way be disposed of.

Three different methods have been devised for getting rid of these troublesome factors. One is that of a scoffing deism, which sets aside the supernatural by imputing it to deception and priestcraft. It is all held to be traceable to impositions practised upon the credulity of the uninstructed vulgar in order to exalt the ministers of religion in their eyes, perhaps for the promotion of selfish ends, perhaps with the worthier motive of obtaining sanction for useful institutions or gaining credence for valuable teachings, which they could not otherwise have been induced so easily to receive. It is only men who are devoid of moral earnestness themselves, and cannot appreciate moral earnestness in others, who can rest satisfied with such an explanation. It is so manifestly opposed to the whole spirit and tenor of the sacred writings, and to the character of the great leaders of Israel, that it has never had any prevalence among those who had any sympathy with, or a just conception of, the men of the Bible. It was soon cast off, therefore, by those who made any pretension to real scholarship, and left to frivolous scoffers.

A second mode of dealing with the supernatural, without admitting its reality, is that of the old rationalistic exegesis. This regards it simply as oriental exaggeration. It is looked upon as the habit of the period to think and speak in superlatives, and to employ grandiloquent figures and forms of expression. In order to ascertain the actual meaning of the writer these must be reduced to the proportion of ordinary events. Thus Eichhorn, the father of the higher criticism, had no difficulty in accepting the Mosaic authorship of the Pentateuch, and defending its credibility, while at the same time he discarded the miraculous. This work, he contended, must be interpreted in accordance with the spirit of the age to which it belonged. Its poetic embellishments must not be mistaken for plain prose, and its bold figures must not be converted into literal statements. When the oriental imagery is duly estimated, and the elaborate drapery in which the imaginative writer has dressed his thought is stripped off, it will be found that his real meaning does not transcend what is purely natural. There was nothing miraculous about the plagues of Egypt; it was only an *annus mirabilis*, a year of extraordinary occurrences, remarkable in their number and severity, but wholly traceable to natural causes. There was nothing miraculous in the passage of the Red Sea, or the events at Sinai, or in what took place during the forty years in the desert. The apparently miraculous features belong merely to the style of description, not to the facts described. There was in this no intentional falsehood, no attempt to deceive. It was the well-understood way of writing and speaking in that age. And thus the supernatural is evaporated by hermeneutical rules. But this unnatural style of interpretation could not long maintain itself. The attempt to reduce heathen myths to intelligible history, and to bring down the miracles of the Bible to the level of ordinary occurrences, proved alike abortive. The hypothesis of rhetorical exaggeration, fashionable as it was at one time, was accordingly abandoned. The rule of common-sense must be applied to Scripture as to any other book, that the writer must be understood to mean what he says, not what some interpreter may fancy that he ought to have said.

The third mode of banishing the supernatural from the Bible is by subjecting it to the processes of the higher criticism. This is the most plausible as well as the most effective method of accomplishing this result. It is the most plausible because the animus of the movement is concealed, and the desired end is reached not by aiming at it directly and avowedly, but as the apparently incidental consequence of investigations pursued professedly for a different purpose. And it is the most effective because it supplies a complete antidote for the supernatural in each of its forms. Every reported miracle is met by the allegation that the record dates centuries after its supposed occurrence, leaving ample time for the legendary amplification of natural events. Every prediction which has been so accurately fulfilled that it cannot be explained away as a vague anticipation, shrewd conjecture, or fortunate coincidence, is met by the allegation that it was not committed to writing till after the event. Revelations of truth in advance of what the unaided faculties of men could be supposed to have attained to must be reconstructed into accordance with the requirements of a gradual scheme of development. The stupendous miracles of the Mosaic period, the far-reaching predictions of the Pentateuch, and its minute and varied legislation are all provided for by the critical analysis, which parts it into separate documents and assigns these documents severally to six, eight, and ten centuries after the exodus from Egypt.

These critical results are based professedly on purely literary grounds, on diction and style and correspondence with historical surroundings. And yet he who traces the progress of critical opinion will discover that these are invariably subordinated to the end of neutralizing the supernatural, and that they are so managed as to lead up to this conclusion. The development of critical hypotheses inimical to the genuineness and the truth of the books of the Bible has from the beginning been in the hands of those who were antagonistic to supernatural religion, whose interest in the Bible was purely literary, and who refused to recognize its claims as an immediate and authoritative revelation from God. These hypotheses, which are largely speculative and conjectural, are to a great extent based upon and shaped by unproved assumptions of the falsity of positive scriptural statements. They are in acknowledged variance with the historical truth of much of the Bible, and require, as is freely confessed, the complete reconstruction of the sacred history. They require us to suppose that the course of events and the progress of divine revelation must throughout have been very different from the representations of the Bible.

Within a very few years professedly evangelical men have ventured upon the hazardous experiment of attempting a compromise in this matter. They propose to accept these hypotheses in spite of their antibiblical character, in spite of their incompatibility with the historical truth of the Bible, in spite of their contravening its explicit statements, in spite of the grave questions which they raise respecting the fallibility of our Lord's own teaching; and they expect to retain their Christian faith with only such modifications as these newly adopted hypotheses may require. They are now puzzling themselves over the problem of harmonizing Christ's sanction

12

given to false views respecting the Old Testament with implicit faith in him as a divine teacher. And some of them in their perplexity over this enigma come perilously near impairing the truth of his claims. Would it not be wiser for them to revise their own ill-judged alliance with the enemies of evangelical truth, and inquire whether Christ's view of the Old Testament may not, after all, be the true view?

INDEX

serviceable to the cause of truth, 132, 133 ; elaborated in the interest of unbelief, 157, 165 ; acceptance by evangelical scholars does not neutralize their pernicious tendencies, 166, 177

Patriarchal period, 20

Pentateuch, its position in the plan of the Old Testament, 8, 9, 13 ; its plan and contents, 18 sqq. ; how denominated, derivation of the word, antiquity of the quintuple division, names of the several books, 18 ; its theme, two principal sections, 19, 36 ; tabulated, 30 ; its importance, 31 ; written by Moses, 32–46 ; claims to be from Moses, 36–39 ; alluded to in later books of the Bible, 52–58, note ; its unity, 59 sqq.; process of its formation according to the critics, 159, 160

People of God, ideas involved in, 21 ; two stages, the family and the nation, 24

Perspicacity claimed by the critics, 126, 127

Peyrerius, 48

Plautus, 129, note

Poetical books, their place in the plan of the Old Testament, 8, 9, 14

Positive types, 11

Postdiluvian period, its aim, 20, 21

Predictions denied or explained away, 165

Predictive periods negative and positive, 12, 13

Priest code, 36, 136–140, 145, 146, 148, 155

Prodigal son, parable of, partitioned, 119–122

Promises to the patriarchs, 24

Prophecies in the Old Testament, their distribution, 11

Prophetical books, their place in the plan of the Old Testament, 9, 14

Psalms, allusions to the Pentateuch, 56, note

RANKE, F. H., 76 and note

Rationalistic exegesis, 174, 175

Redactor proposed by Gramberg, 63, note ; inconsistencies imputed to him in Hupfeld's hypothesis, 86, 87 ; deals arbitrarily with the text, 91 sqq., 161, 163, 168–170 ; his mode of compiling the Pentateuch, 159, 160 ; not infallibly inspired, 168

Religion of the Bible based on historical facts, 165

Rephidim, narrative of the battle there recorded by Moses, 37, 38

Reuss, 142, note

Revealed religion antagonized by critical hypotheses, 164 sqq.

Revelations of truth denied or explained away, 165

Robertson, Professor J., 143, note

Romans Dissected, 125

Rupprecht, 142, note

Ruth, its position in the order of the canon, 6, 7 ; allusions to the Pentateuch, 52, note

SACRIFICES elsewhere than at the sanctuary and by others than priests, 150–153

Samaritan, the Good, parable of, partitioned, 122–125